DON VALLEY LEGACY
A PIONEER HISTORY

DON VALLEY LEGACY
A PIONEER HISTORY

by
ANN GUTHRIE

THE BOSTON MILLS PRESS

CANADIAN CATALOGUING IN PUBLICATION DATA

Guthrie, Ann
　Don Valley Legacy — A Pioneer History

Includes bibliographical references.
ISBN 0-919783-15-5

1. Taylor family.　2. Don Valley (Toronto, Ont.) — History.　I. Title.

FC3097.52.G87 1985　971.3'541　C86-093026-2
F1059.5. T686D65 1985

© Ann Guthrie, 1986

Published by:
THE BOSTON MILLS PRESS
132 Main Street
Erin, Ontario N0B 1T0
(519) 833-2407

Designed by Gill Stead
Typeset by Lexigraf, Tottenham
Printed by Ampersand, Guelph

Major funding for this project was provided by the Ontario Heritage Foundation, Ontario Ministry of Citizenship and Culture.

We wish to acknowledge the financial support and encouragement of The Canada Council, the Ontario Arts Council and the Office of the Secretary of State.

Contents

Foreword		7
Preface		9
I.	Emigration and Settlement	17
II.	Early Years in the Don Valley	27
III.	The Daughters	55
IV.	From Yeomen to Manufacturers	79
V.	Prosperity	107
VI.	William Taylor and the Don Valley Pressed Brick Works	135
VII.	The Davies	161
VIII.	Taylor v. Davies	189

FOREWORD

The increasing interest in the history of Toronto and genealogical research provided the impetus for this book on the Taylor family, who lived in East York and the vicinity of Toronto, and on the historical development of the Don Valley. I was encouraged by the East York Historical Society, who were interested in the history of the family and the contribution it made to the development of the Township in the nineteenth century, and by Mrs. Eleanor Darke, the former Curator of the Todmorden Mills Museum. Without her assistance and that of my husband, H. Donald Guthrie, Q.C., my daughter Gay and my son Neil, this book would not have been possible.

I am also indebted to many others who listened and provided me with information: my daughter Barbara, Miss Jessica V. Taylor and Dr. Edith Taylor; Mrs. George C. Gale; Mr. and Mrs. George T. Gale; Dr. Ronald R. Tasker; Mr. and Mrs. Walter Taylor; Mr. Gordon Davies; Mr. Douglas Davies; Mrs. Arthur Haywood; Mr. and Mrs. N. Defries; Mrs. Kathryn Dowthwaite; Miss Edna Ash; Mrs. Robert Abbott; Mrs. Cosby Lamont; Mrs. Adele Davies Rockwell; Mrs. E.G. Legrice; Mr. Peter Mayor and Mrs. Guelph Mayor; Mrs. Helen Schwab; Mr. Ian Howes; and Mrs. Mary Lloyd of the Richmond Hill Public Library.

The family tree was begun by Mrs. Dorothy Milne, and Mr. Ross Wallace gave me his research on the family of Thomas Taylor. My father-in-law, Mr. Donald Guthrie, Q.C., prepared a summary of the law reports of *Taylor v. Davies*. Two cousins, Miss Jessica Taylor and Mrs. George C. Gale, were particularly helpful and provided me with many details about the family before they both died in 1977. I have listened to members of the family relate their reminiscences for years and was fortunate to have inherited a collection of family papers, photographs, portraits and scrapbooks—but regrettably there are no Taylor diaries, journals or letters in the collection. The scattered references to the family and its enterprises in books and periodicals have not always been accurate and I have endeavoured to rectify this failure by using church records, the Registry Office, the Ontario Archives and pamphlets and newspapers of the day. I am grateful for the assistance of the staffs of all the Toronto-based archives that have made my research so much easier.

Finally, I would like to thank the Ontario Heritage Foundation of the Ontario Ministry of Citizenship and Culture for its financial and technical support in producing this book. The Ministry's choice of Neil Semple as editor was fortunate for me and I would like to express my gratitude to him for his careful editing of the text.

PREFACE

When Governor John Graves Simcoe came to the site of the future city of Toronto, he found only a small settlement of about two hundred people clustered along Lake Ontario. A large peninsula created a beautiful natural harbour and to the east and west respectively, the Don and Humber Rivers dissected the lake plain and created natural barriers to settlement. The Don River consisted of many small tributaries and two main branches which joined approximately five miles north of Lake Ontario at what was called the Forks of the Don. Dr. Henry Scadding gives us perhaps the best description of what the Don Valley was like before 1830. He described springs that gushed from the hillsides, dense forests of magnificent trees and a profusion of "high shrubbery of wild willow, alder, wych-hazel, dog-wood, tree-cranberry . . . interwoven in numerous places with the vine of wild grape".[1] He spoke of the "innumerable" wild animals that left their foot-prints in the snow and "night-fishing excursions on the Don when in the course of an hour some twenty heavy salmon were speared".[2]

The valley, which is approximately a quarter of a mile wide, has been drastically altered over the last two centuries, but in Scadding's time it was distinguished by deep ravines, thickly wooded hillsides and stretches of beautiful meadows and marshes through which the river meandered. At its mouth, near the base of the peninsula that formed the town's great harbour, the broad marshland extended for acres and to the east were the cliffs that reminded the Simcoes of Scarborough in Yorkshire.

Both the Humber and the Don provided important sources for water power that greatly influenced the future development of the region. Governor Simcoe early recognized the importance of mills to the Province and when the first Parliament of Upper

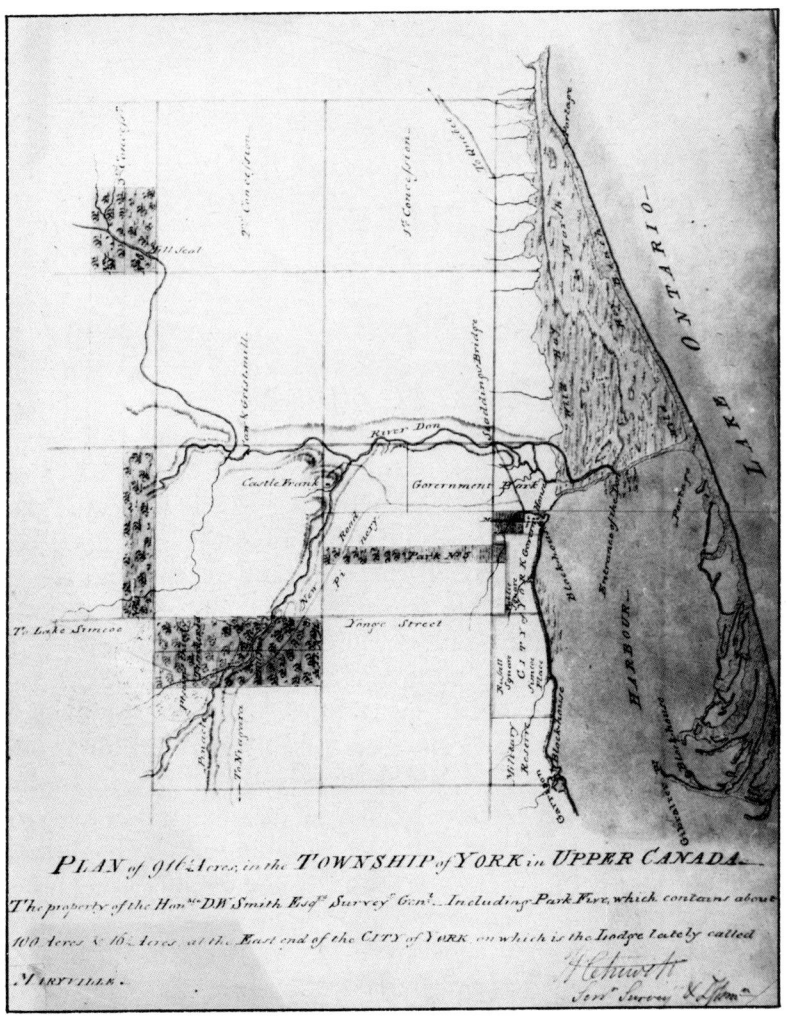

The Don River, 1790s
Todmorden Mills Archives

Canada met in 1793, it removed the restrictions hindering their growth. Anyone who wanted to build a mill on his property was permitted to do so providing that he did not "thereby prejudice the navigation or obstruct the passage of fish in those waters".[3] The first sawmill was built near the mouth of the Humber, but it soon proved inadequate and another site closer to York was sought.

The Don River
Historical Atlas of York County, Miles and Company 1878

John Coon, an early settler in the Don Valley, claimed that he had the right to a millsite, but, perhaps because of his poor business reputation, it was granted to Isaiah Skinner. The primitive one-storey mill that Skinner erected on Lot 13, Concession 11[4] was completed in the spring of 1795. Simcoe himself built a summer residence, "Castle Frank", on a steep hill overlooking the Don Valley near the present intersection of Parliament and Bloor Streets using lumber from the Skinner mill. Mrs. Simcoe, who loved to entertain at Castle Frank, often visited the Skinner mill.

In 1796, Skinner was also given permission to build a grist mill. It was the only one near York and as traffic to his mill grew, a better road was necessary. John Small and William Willcox,

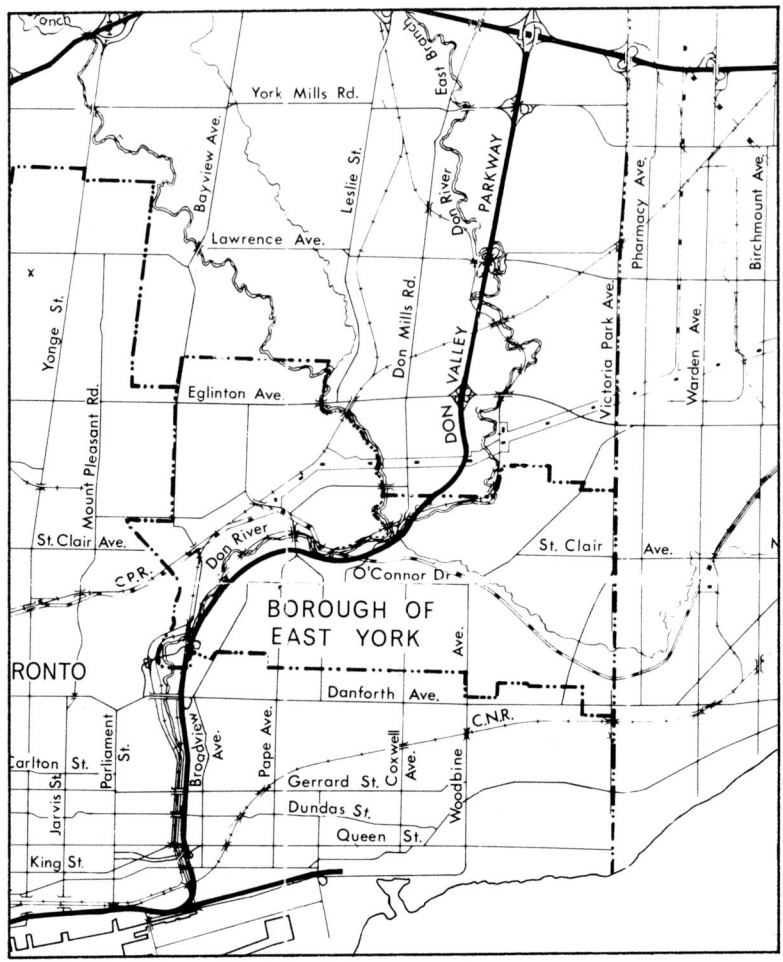

The Don River showing the Don Valley Parkway and the Borough of East York.
Metropolitan Toronto Library Board

therefore, signed an order requesting Isaiah Skinner's father Timothy to "proceed to open a road on the other side of the Bridge (at Queen Street) to your mills in the best manner and most convenient place you can". [5] It was little more than a trail wide enough for a wagon hewn through the dense pine woods on the east side of the valley, but it remained the principal road for the area until 1841. It was called the Don Mills Road and today Broadview Avenue follows the same route. Parshall Terry built another mill farther up the Don in 1799 and extended the Don Mills Road to it. In fact, the first official mention of Don Mills is in the title given to James Playter in 1799, "Overseer of Highways from the Bay Road to Don Mills". [6]

Don Mills Road significantly improved access to the southeast part of York. This area was originally set aside in the town plans for government buildings. Although some construction was begun at the foot of Berkeley Street, the buildings were never completed. However, a good part of the town's business section was located in this area and in 1803 five and a half acres were designated for a market. The road also opened up the large property granted to John Scadding on the east side of the Don. Scadding had been brought out in 1792 by Simcoe as his estate manager and was given the land from the lake to Danforth Avenue.

Except for 1797, when "the Inhabitants of the Don and Marsh" were numbered at 35 men and 34 women, the actual population in the Don Valley cannot be ascertained from official records. After that date, they were included in the figures for York and Scarborough. In 1812, this represented only 756 people, but by 1820 the number had grown to 1,240. The population reached 9,252 by 1834 when the town of York became the city of Toronto. By this time, the main thrust of development had turned west toward the Garrison Common and north above Queen Street. Even though the city gradually consolidated as the century progressed and settlement reached north to Bloor Street and west to Dufferin, the Don Valley remained essentially rural until well after 1900.

However, small villages did form along the Don Mills Road including Don Mount, near Queen Street, then Doncaster, and north of Danforth Avenue, Chester, and Todmorden at the intersection with Pottery Road. The families of Eastwoods and Helliwells, who built houses, a brewery, distillery and a paper mill near Skinner's mills, named the area Todmorden after their original home in Yorkshire. William Helliwell, who came to the valley from Niagara in 1820, described the area as a hunter's and a fisherman's paradise. He said that his father-in-law, Thomas Bright, "bagged 30 or 40 ducks in the marsh at the foot of the Don in an afternoon after his business at the market was over". [7] He wrote in his Memorandums that,

The Don River,
Author's collection

In the spring of the year, the river was literally alive with suckers where they were caught and carried away by the waggon load and in the autumn salmon were almost as numerous weighing from 10 to 20 pounds each . . . In the spring vast quantities of pigeons used to be flying to their breeding grounds and for days and even weeks the sun was almost darkened by the immense flocks that were flying and at street corners and points of hills people assembled with guns and poured into the flocks as they passed by the deadly shot, killing great numbers of them . . . [7]

As the nineteenth century progressed, the land in the north end of the valley was cleared and farmed, the trees were cut for lumber and more mills were built by enterprising pioneer families.

One family—the Taylors—who settled at the Forks of the Don were eventually responsible for much of the economic development of the area. It is important for the history of the locality, as well as for the heritage of the City of Toronto, that their achievements be recognized. Beginning with only a small farm in 1831, they amassed a land holding of nearly 4,000 acres, started grist, saw and paper mills on the Don and eventually built a huge brick-making operation. The Taylors also helped to found one of Canada's principal banks, were a major employer in the region and contributed to the religious and educational needs of the local citizens. This is their story.

Notes

1. Henry Scadding, *Toronto of Old,* edited by F.H. Armstrong (Toronto: Oxford University Press, 1966), p. 159.
2. *Ibid.,* p. 161.
3. Metropolitan Toronto Public Library, (hereafter MTPL), Minutes of the Executive Council, 16 April, 1793.
4. Department of Planning and Development, *Don Valley Conservation Report* Historical section by V.B. Black, (Toronto: 1950), p. 70.
5. (TMA), E. Darke and I. Wheal, "Todmorden Mills: a Nineteenth-Century Mill Town," (n.p., n.d.), p. 9. One of the principal sources of information on the early mills in the Don Valley is an unpublished paper in the Todmorden Mills Archives by Eleanor Darke and Ian Wheal, "Todmorden Mills: a Nineteenth-Century Mill Town".
6. Baldwin Room, MTPL, (hereafter BR), Minutes of Town Meetings, 1792-1822, March 1799.
7. (BR), Memorandums of William Helliwell, pp. 13-14.

John Taylor 1771/3-1866/8
Author's collection

I
EMIGRATION AND SETTLEMENT

The Taylor family left England during the 1820s along with thousands of other families who sought new opportunities abroad. In the wake of the great depression which followed the Napoleonic Wars, Great Britain suffered under a heavy public debt, displaced trade and industry, a rapid population growth, and increasing rural dislocation through land enclosures. Emigration was advocated by many, including William Horton, the Under-Secretary for War and the Colonies, as the most expedient solution to the increasing poverty at home. By 1826, when a select committee of the House of Commons reported that "a redundancy of able-bodied people were living in a state of pauperism", the exodus from the British Isles was well under way. [1]

At the same time, there was an almost insatiable demand for information about Britain's colonies, and letters, journals and lecturers from abroad poured into the country for this receptive audience. Little was left untold as the climate, the towns, the people, the living and working conditions were all described in minute detail. Even such criticisms as that of one author writing in 1821, who saw "even in the oldest settlements ... a state of primitive rudeness and barbarism" [2] had little dampening effect on the appeal of a new life with the promise of greater opportunity.

Such an exodus entailed the dispersal of possessions, except for the necessities and perhaps a few precious treasures, and farewells to relatives and friends; but most prepared to leave with cheerfulness. They were certain that their decision to make a new life in a new country was the right one. Many set out for the United States for the simple reason that more ships sailed to New York and other American ports than to Quebec, and they were more comfortable and better appointed. Others went there because economic opportunity was greater than in Canada. Many stayed, but some moved north later, preferring the security of the British system of government which they had known at home.

It is a wonder that so many survived the trip and arrived at all. The ships in which they travelled were called by one author "puny vehicles"[3] of 300 to 400 tons, which had disposed of their cargoes of cotton, tobacco or lumber from the new world in British ports. For the return voyage, the hold was filled with casks of water and heavy baggage. Above this was the steerage accommodation for passengers, which was all that most could afford. Here several hundred were crowded into a space six feet high, with two tiers of berths around the sides, each wide enough for five people to sleep on, and a small central floor space. Before embarking, it was the practice for passengers to bargain on the docks for the cost of their passage which amounted to between £2/10 and £4 per person, although it was possible for a family to negotiate a better price for "the whole in a lump".[4] The travellers supplied their own provisions, which they cooked on primitive stoves made out of half a barrel lined with bricks and covered with a grill and set out on the open decks, or on the stove in the galley for which they had to wait their turn.

Two other types of vessels offered better accommodation for those who could afford it. One carried second-class passengers who paid £1 extra for a separate "room" formed by a partition of thin boards which separated them from the steerage and made life a little more bearable by giving some privacy. However, it was generally accepted that "no one will think the better or worse of them on account of the part of the ship in which they chanced to come", and the really worthy and discerning were held in "higher esteem for their economy".[5] The packet, the other type of vessel which plied the Atlantic during those years, was the name given to the eighteenth century ships that travelled between Britain and the colonies. The term was later used to describe those ships carrying cargoes of mail, light freight and cabin passengers. These passengers paid from 30 to 40 guineas for their accommodation, but they were few in comparison to the majority who came by steerage, despite the often fatal hardships which they endured.

Although the emigrants had been warned about conditions on the ships, and knew how long the voyage would take, few realized the extent of the discomfort awaiting them. Water was in short supply and it was almost impossible to keep clean. The over-crowding added to the prevalence of serious, contagious diseases such as typhus, cholera, measles, dysentery, small pox, and the general malaise of ship-fever, from which many died. There was little to do on board ship, brawls and thefts were common, children ran everywhere and when storms lashed the Atlantic, sea-chests crashed from their fastenings and nerves were shattered by the creaking and groaning of the ship and the cries of the passengers. But when land was sighted at last, the unpleasantness was forgotten; music and singing broke out and hearts gladdened as the ship moved up the Hudson River to New York.

The entrance to New York by ship has always been an impressive sight and early travellers from Europe were awed by the beauty of the hills and magnificent trees of the land that was to be their new home. Once they were in the harbour, all the excitement of arrival began as the ship was surrounded by small craft from which the travel-weary passengers were opportuned to buy clothes, food and trinkets. Even land and jobs were offered to them while they were still on board ship. Prices were four times more on the seaboard than anywhere else and after disembarking no one stayed long in lodgings. Mary Gapper, who later lived in Vaughan Township, wrote in her diary that when she arrived in 1820, she was fortunate enough to be conducted by the captain to a boarding house at one end of the famous Broadway where she enjoyed the meals but was critical of the implements with which to eat them. [6]

In January of 1833, William Helliwell, one of the earliest residents of Toronto's Don Valley and Todmorden Mills, wrote in his diary that he had ridden his new horse through the woods to see what was going on "out that way" and had found the Sinclairs and the Taylors cutting out new roads. On the way home, he

> took a new road and followed the bank of the Don from Thorne's feild to the top of the hill above Tailor's new house where I disended and passed through Tailor's wheat field. [7]*

This is the earliest known reference to the Taylor family in the story of the development of York and the Don Valley.

In 1821, John Taylor, his wife and children sailed from England to New York, but as with countless emigrants of humble background who left the British Isles to start a new life in America, very little is known about this period in their lives. Later, members of the third generation of the family wrote conflicting accounts of those early years which combined fact and recollection. One great grand-daughter, Jessica V. Taylor, wrote that the voyage took thirteen weeks and that John's wife, Margaret Hawthorne, died and was buried at sea, while another stated that the voyage took only seven weeks and that Margaret died in 1824 in Cherry Valley, New York, where the family first settled. Other members of the family thought that there were nine children in the family, but only seven—four daughters and three sons—can be documented.

At the time that they left England, the oldest child, Mary, was twenty-one, Elizabeth was sixteen, Edith fourteen and Margaret, the youngest, was four. The three sons, John, Thomas and George, were boys of twelve, ten and eight years respectively. It is known from the headstones in the Taylor cemetery (which is located at the west side of Don Mills United Church) at the corner of Pape and Broadview Avenues, that the family came from Uttoxeter, Staffordshire, when John Sr. was about forty-eight years of age. Unfortunately, the monument on his grave has eroded badly and it is unclear whether he was born in 1771 or 1773, but it is evident that he was not a young man to be starting a new life in a pioneer country.

It was not uncommon for immigrants to leave New York City via the Hudson River, a pleasant voyage of one hundred and fifty miles of clear sailing. Those who could afford it travelled by steamship, but the majority went by barges which were towed by tugs. John Taylor and his family got as far as Cherry Valley in the Finger Lakes region where they settled for three years and then, according to Jessica Taylor, John decided that he wanted to be with "his own people" under the British flag. [8] Accompanied by five of his children, he travelled by ox-cart to York by way of Kingston. There, he had been advised that a Mr. Holmes who lived on Yonge Street would help him. The family was supposed to have rented a house which had been occupied

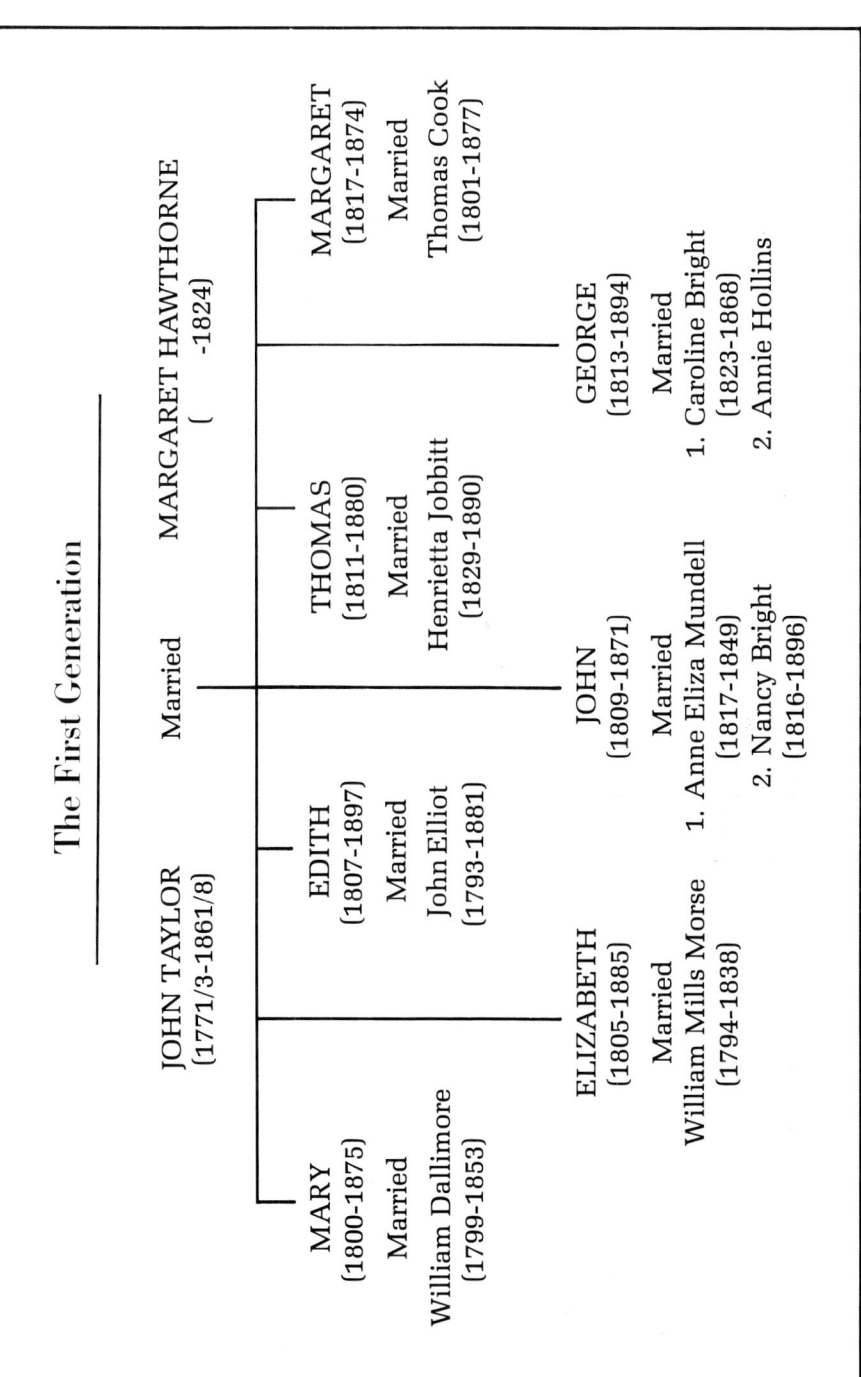

by Governor Simcoe, a distinction which may have appealed to later members of the family but which was most unlikely since the Simcoes lived either in the Governor's military tent or at "Castle Frank". Jessica Taylor also thought that they operated a dairy before they moved to Vaughan Township, north of the city, but this may have been speculation on her part.

When the Taylors arrived in York in 1825, it was a small community of 1,685 people with 225 wooden houses and 39 stores. The streets were laid out in the standard grid pattern; settlement was still largely to the east of Yonge Street towards the Don Valley and the main centre of activity was at the edge of the lake. Early writers spoke of the beauty of the harbour and the natural setting of the town, but despaired of the surrounding swampy areas and the lack of defences in time of war. [9] Roads and communications to the out-lying areas were limited, but York was becoming a prosperous regional centre as more people arrived. The town was the capital of Upper Canada and a major military outpost. It was also an important agricultural centre and it would not have taken John Taylor long to learn that he should look for land in Vaughan Township. Situated only sixteen miles northwest of York, it was clearly the place to make money. Crops were excellent due to a fortunate combination of climate and good soil, and much of the land had already been cleared.

This area, with which the Taylors were associated for three successive generations, had an interesting background. Very early, Vaughan had been notorious for land speculation by two men in particular, Captain Richard Lippincott and Captain Daniel Cozens. They had each been granted approximately 3,000 acres for their services to the Crown during the American Revolution, but they were not settlers and were prepared to sell their land to the highest bidder. At about the same time, Governor Simcoe decided to encourage a group of German settlers from Pennsylvania to come to Canada and advertised in the Philadelphia newspapers offering free land. Although this offer was withdrawn when he was recalled to England in 1796, it provided the impetus for the migration of German families who continued to travel across the border in their Conestoga wagons well into the nineteenth century. Dissatisfied with life in the United States, where land became too expensive for them to buy farms for their sons, they came to Canada to join relatives and friends.

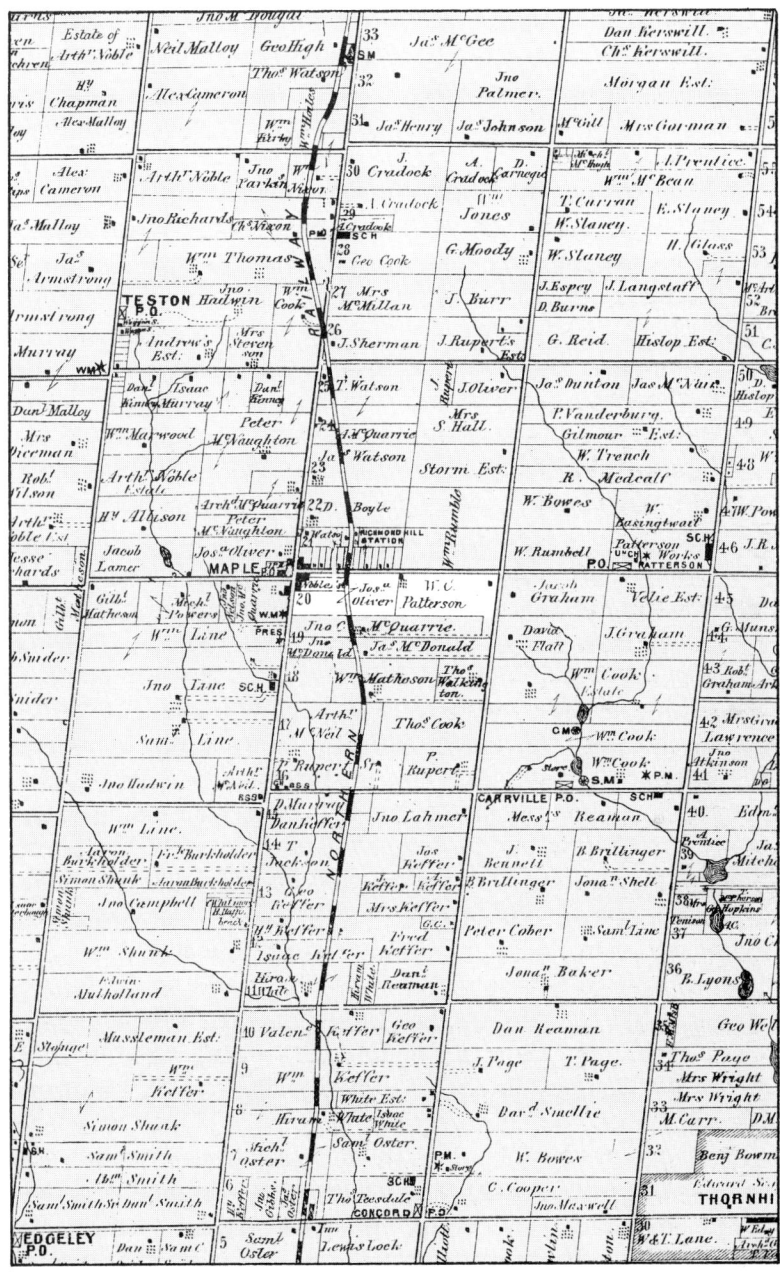

Vaughan Township, showing Mr. Taylor's property, Lot 20, Concession III.
Historical Atlas of York County, Miles and Company, 1878

Many settled in Vaughan and bought land from the two captains. The German migration is part of the heritage of Vaughan Township today where names like Reesor, Reaman, Burkholder, Billinger, Hilts, Troyer, Keefer, Snider and Fisher recall these early settlers.

Another aspect of land settlement at that time was that by the 1820s, the government of Sir Peregrine Maitland had decided to change its policy of land grants. Generally speaking, Crown patents were offered to only two groups, the military and the United Empire Loyalists. This was done deliberately so that only those immigrants with money could obtain land, leaving the poorer ones to form part of a labour pool which would alleviate the shortage of hired help and promote industrial development. Most government land was in the outlying areas and although cheaper, many still preferred to buy either from absentee owners, from the Canada Company in southwestern Ontario, or from those who were moving elsewhere since this land was usually closer to the main towns and had been partially cleared.

John Taylor purchased a hundred acre farm in Vaughan from John and Mary Smeldzter in November 1825 for £137/10. [10] The Smeldzters [11] moved north to King Township with their six children and the Taylors farmed the land they had bought from them for the next six years. Nothing is known about the Taylor family during this period, but it is apparent from the family genealogy that John never remarried and that his two oldest daughters, Mary and Elizabeth, were married about the time the family settled in Vaughan. Their sister Edith was eighteen, old enough to be in charge of the household, and young John at sixteen could have helped his father on the farm. The three youngest children, Thomas, George and Margaret, were of school age but for the boys, farm work took priority over education and only when they were not needed at home would they have been permitted to attend school. In those days, rural education was limited and one of the old-time residents of Vaughan, Jonathan Baker, described it as he remembered it. In his memoirs, he wrote that a teacher first went around the countryside looking for pupils and when he found enough to pay his salary, started a school in whatever building was available. Sometimes it was a private house, a meeting-house, or, in Baker's case, the carpenter's shop on his father's property.[12] This was adequate for most and was all the formal education that they received.

The Taylors lived in Vaughan until 1831 when the farm was sold for £200.[13] John was then sixty years of age. Farming was profitable and it would have been a good place for him to end his days, except the hundred acre farm had little to offer his three sons. They were young men ready for more opportunity and thus the Taylors moved east to the Don Valley. For £92, which was a good price, they bought 82 acres and acquired land that was both close to York and had the added advantage of a stretch of the Don River running through it.[14] This was an important consideration in the early days of settlement when water power went hand in hand with clearing the land and gave the settlers the means to set up their own saw and grist mills.

This was an important move for it was here that the family would make its fortune. In the years that followed, the three sons more than justified their parents' decision to emigrate from Staffordshire and it was because of their enterprise that much of the township of East York was developed.

Notes

1. G.F. Plant, *Overseas Development* (Oxford: Oxford University Press, 1951), p. 24.
2. J. Howison, *Sketches of Upper Canada* (York: W. Lettaker, 1821; reprinted, Coles Publishing, 1970), p. 68.
3. M.L. Hanson, *The Immigrant in American History* (Boston: Harvard University Press, 1940), p. 181.
4. *Ibid.*, p. 49.
5. E.C. Guillet, *The Great Migration* (Toronto: Nelson & Assoc., 1937), p. 52.
6. M.L. Hanson, pp. 188-189.
7. (TMA), Helliwell Diaries, 2 January, 1833.
8. Jessica V. Taylor, letters to the author.
9. J. Howison, pp. 35-36.
10. Registry Office, Old York Book E., Part I, c64-3, p. 539, Rear half of Lot 20, Concession 3, Vaughan Township.

11. *The History of the County of York,* (Toronto: C. Blackett Robinson, 1885), 2 v., v. II, p. 421. The spelling is recorded as Smelser. "The Smeldzers, as their name would indicate, were Germans from Pennsylvania who had emigrated earlier and had become such good citizens that John was even awarded a medal for his 'fidelity and bravery' when he fought in the War of 1812 against his former countrymen."
12. (Richmond Hill Public Library, henceforth RHPL), Memoirs of Jonathan Baker (unpublished, 1896) Scrapbook #1, "A brief history of the early settlers on this line . . . ", p. 81.
13. Registry Office, #7790, Vaughan Township.
14. Registry Office, #9326, Lot II, Concession 3, F.B.

* All quotations have been left in their original spelling and form.

II

EARLY YEARS IN THE DON VALLEY

William Helliwell's reference to the Taylor family in January 1833 comes a year after he began a series of diaries which he was to continue writing at intervals until 1887. With no Taylor diaries extant, Helliwell's record of all the families that formed the community of Todmorden remains one of the most valuable documents of those early years in the Don Valley. Helliwell seems to have been a compulsive diarist, recording all that he saw, but unfortunately only six of his volumes have survived and these are in the archives of Todmorden Mills Museum. The museum is located on the site of his house at the foot of Pottery Road hill in East York. The volumes contain many references to the Taylors and others of the Todmorden circle—and Helliwell continued his association with these families even after he moved to Pickering Township in 1847. Much of the diaries' charm lies in Helliwell's sometimes erratic spelling and grammar and the very graphic style in which he frames his narrative. This delightful and original quality is maintained in this book whenever quotations are drawn from his diaries.

William Helliwell's family came from a manufacturing background in Todmorden, Yorkshire, England, where his father Thomas owned a cotton manufacturing company before he immigrated to Upper Canada in 1818. William Helliwell described it in his memoirs:

> *My father was a small cotton manufacturer and also occupied and owned a small farm. At that time there were no power looms, the manufacturer only spinning the cotton and the weavers taking the yarn and weaving it into calico by hand looms. Every stream that afforded a power sufficient to drive a spinning and carding machine was utilized. This*

Todmorden, Yorkshire, England
National Geographic

was before the advent of steam. After carding and spinning, the yarn was given out to weavers who took it home and wove it into calico and returned it to the "Cotton Masters" who took it to Manchester or Halifax to large capitalists who bleached, printed and fitted it for exportation. In this way the manufacturing industry came to be in England. [1]

During that period, the introduction of a centralized, large-scale factory system in England forced many small manufacturers out of business and a large number decided to leave the country. However, Thomas Helliwell was prohibited from leaving because he was classed as a skilled manufacturer and he was forced to depart alone, in secret. He joined his son-in-law John Eastwood (who had married his daughter Betty) in the District of Niagara. They lived at the corner of Lundy's Lane and the Queenston Road at what is now Drummondville. [2] Thomas Helliwell's wife and six children came out from England the following year and the two families operated a general store together for a short time.

Todmorden Mills
Beautiful Canada, 1896

Within a year, the Helliwells had rented a distillery nearby and it became part of the on-going family tradition that "grain taken in payment for goods at the store was shipped to the distillery, made into whiskey and sold back to the store's customers". [3] It was a profitable business since in rural areas there were sometimes one or more taverns per mile. [4] Many settlers depended on whisky to relieve the tedium of endless work and the hardships which they had to endure. Excessive drinking was one of the common hazards of pioneer life.

By 1821, the Helliwells and the Eastwoods decided to move to the Don Valley where they purchased ten acres of land from the Skinner family. [5] Thomas's son William, accompanied by John and Betty Eastwood, recorded that they went on ahead and

> . . . made the Don Mills in one day but Mother and the remainder of the family removed from the Falls during the winter, Mother riding in a large brewing kettle purchased from Clark and Street and which was used for many a year in the Don Brewery and was afterwards sold to Alexander Milne for a dye kettle in his woollen factory. [6]

Sarah Lord Helliwell
Todmorden Mills Archives

    The family lived in a small frame house and nearby Thomas Helliwell built a small brewery, a malt house, and a distillery. It was an historic site, for in 1795-1796 Isaiah Skinner had built his mills there. Eastwood and Thomas Helliwell had agreed to go into partnership in the mills with Skinner's son Colin, who had moved from Niagara to settle on another part of the property at about the same time. However, the partnership was short-lived because Helliwell preferred to carry on with his brewing and distilling. Later Eastwood and Skinner converted the old mills into a paper mill.

    It was natural for them to call their little settlement Todmorden after their home in Yorkshire and this name continued to be used for nearly a hundred years. It never officially became a village although the name was commonly used in the Toronto Directories to describe the junction area of Don Mills Road, or Broadview Avenue as it became, and Pottery Road in East York.

    The Helliwells were successful businessmen and when Thomas died in 1825 his wife Sarah Lord carried on the business with her sons. One of the sons, Thomas Jr., lived in York where he bought grain and sold beer. In 1828, he obtained an important concession when he was granted on petition one of the few water lots in the harbour. Here he built a large shipping wharf. [7]

William and Joseph Helliwell
Todmorden Mills Archives

William and his brother Joseph lived at the mills which Henry Scadding described as "a secluded spot" with "bears, wolves and deer moving about in the adjacent forest". [8] William Helliwell told Scadding that "one night wolves killed a dozen of his sheep, one of them being killed on the doorstep" and that "returning one day from the town, he came upon a huge bear in the road near the Don Bridge." [9]

Todmorden Mills Archives

Helliwell House, built 1825-1838, photographed in 1934 before restoration.
Todmorden Mills Archives

Joseph Helliwell lived in a small frame house not far from the brewery until 1835 when he exchanged it with his brother for the family stone house. In 1838, William added a two-storey mud-brick section to the frame house. This house has been restored at Todmorden Mills. Both brothers needed large dwellings to house their growing families. Their wives were expected to care for a lively household of young children and at the same time be "active, industrious, ingenious, cheerful and not above putting a hand to whatever was necessary to be done in the household." [10] Joseph's first wife had ten children and found solace praying in her cupboard and writing about her religious experiences in her diary, but William's wife, whom he married when she was nineteen, lacked the stamina to survive the birth of six children in less than ten years and died when she was twenty-eight.

William was much shaken by the death of his beloved wife. His diaries describe their courtship and life together as well as his wife's family, the Brights, who are also of particular interest to the Taylors. John and George Taylor married Bright daughters. Thanks to William Helliwell, we have an intimate account of life in York and the Don Valley after 1832. The Taylors, Brights and Helliwells attended many of the same weddings and funerals —the milestones of their lives—and it is apparent from the last diary, written between 1879 and 1887, that their friendship continued until old age.

To avoid possible confusion, it should be explained that there were two families of Brights living in York at this time. One was that of Lewis Bright, a former soldier, who came to York as early as 1797, and the other belonged to Thomas Bright, a butcher. When Lewis Bright died at the distinguished age of ninety-five, the *Toronto Patriot* described him as the oldest resident in Toronto, if not in Upper Canada. Born in 1747 in Gloucestershire, England, Lewis had sailed for America with the 47th Regiment of Foot in 1775. He served at the frontier fortresses of Niagara, Detroit and Michilimacinac and went on an expedition to Kentucky "in the course of which five hundred prisoners were captured and forts taken".[11] He was discharged in 1784 and eventually came to York. Later he returned to his military calling with the Royal Canadian Volunteers for service in the War of 1812. As a reward, he was appointed Messenger of the Honourable Legislative Council and in this capacity carried dispatches through the dense forests. But when the Legislature was in session, he proudly stood guard at the door. When he retired from this post at ninety-one years of age he petitioned for a pension (which amounted to £62/10) and cited his services to the Crown during the Rebellion of 1837 as one of the reasons it should be granted:

> *Your petitioner, likewise, turned out on the 4th of December, 1837 and was directed to take charge of the rooms and offices of the Legislative Council, which were then in a state of great confusion from their being occupied by the militia; during his charge of the buildings, nothing was injured and nothing was lost, except for his own fusee, which one of the loyal militia, he believes, took away by mistake . . .* [12]

Helliwell Brewery, photographed in 1934 before restoration.
Todmorden Mills Archives

He also spoke of the large family he and his wife, Margaret Brady had produced.

> Your Excellency's memorialist further begs to state that he is the father of sixteen children, eight sons and eight daughters, and that the taint of disloyalty never attached to his name or race. Three of his sons volunteered to accompany the brave and lamented General Brock to Detroit, and continued under his command until the time of his death . . . [13]

One of his daughters, Susan, married James Austin of "Spadina" [14] and another, Jane, married Charles Scadding, a brother of the historian, Rev. Dr. Henry Scadding. A third daughter, Elizabeth or Betsy as she was called, became the wife of James Jobbitt, a tailor. The Jobbitt's daughter, Henrietta, married Thomas Taylor in 1846. [15]

The Taylors and William Helliwell, however, had a much closer relationship with the family of Thomas Bright, the butcher. In 1815, his name appears as a witness on two documents with Samuel Ridout and Samuel Jarvis, and in 1827 he bought Lot 12, Concession IFB from the Honourable Peter Robinson for £250. In 1829, he purchased Lot 9 on Palace Street for £150 [16] and in Walton's Directory of 1833-1834, he was listed as living on Prince's Street which ran north between Palace and Duke Streets. [17] In 1835, he also subscribed for a "piece of plate" for Dr. John Strachan as a testimonial to his services to the victims of cholera during the spring and summer of 1832. [18]

35

Jane Hunter Bright. Portrait painted by Charles Loeffler, 1863, the year before she died.
Author's collection

Thomas Bright's wife, Jane Hunter, was a more mysterious figure. She never explained to her family why she received pieces of gold from England until her death in 1864. Was she the illegitimate daughter of someone important? Was it remittance money? Unfortunately the mystery was never solved. Jane and her husband Thomas had two sons and at least nine daughters, and their marriages extended the family circle to include some of the important merchant families in York. Their daughter Margaret married William Gooderham, Jr., the eldest son of the patriarch of the Gooderham family who had immigrated to York in 1832 after serving in the British army in the West Indies. [19] He had gone into partnership with James Worts in the flour milling business and Worts' son, James Gooderham Worts, married Sarah Bright, or "Sally" as Helliwell called her. Her sister Harriet married John Wilmot, a tavern keeper in the Garrison. [20] Mary, another sister, became the wife of George Stegman on September 1, 1831. [21] He was a merchant and likely a descendant of John Stegman, the deputy Provincial Surveyor who lost his life along with the Solicitor General, Robert Isaac De Gray, Angus McDonnell and other prominent members of York who were on their way to attend a murder trial in the schooner "Speedy" when it sank off Presqu'il Point in October, 1804. [22] Lucinda Bright married Charles Barber who had a varied career as a wholesale brewer and soap and candle-maker before he started the first potash business in the community. [23] Caroline Bright married George Taylor and Nancy Bright became the second wife of John Taylor when she was thirty-five. Last of all, William Helliwell married first Elizabeth in 1834 and then Jane Bright in 1845.

When Helliwell was courting Elizabeth, he describe his visits to her house in his diary and what could be more entertaining than to read of their celebration on New Year's Day in 1833. He was invited for tea after which a fiddler was called in for dancing, but alas, "Poor Cuffers" (the name that Helliwell gave to the fiddler) had such a "Scarey fit" that after three or four tries he was dismissed and another musician was called in. They danced reels and jigs and country dances until four in the morning when the "company broke up much pleased with themselves and everybody else". The gentlemen carried on with Mr. Willard, [24] who invited George Stegman, William Bright and Helliwell to "take a glass of wine with him". In less than a week, William Helliwell returned to the Bright's where, still in the flush of good humour engendered by the party, he took "some libertys" with Elizabeth and they had words. He parted from her "in a very bad humour" but two days later they were reconciled and he "stopt" with her until half past eight. On the 6th of February of the following year they were married at the Anglican Cathedral.

He was devoted to her and in the diaries always refers to her as his "Dear Girl" or, more formally, as "Mrs. Helliwell". They exchanged many visits with her family and he speaks of driving Mrs. Helliwell in the cart "to take dinner" at the Brights'. In April of 1835, Elizabeth's sisters "Miss Nancy and Salley" came up in the morning to visit them "And as it rained they stopt all night".

Helliwell was very close to his wife's family and that first year of their marriage was an eventful one, full of sadness. The first tragedy occurred during the summer and William was called upon to help.

> This morning I got up early as Mr. Bright intended burying his little Girl at six o'clock—The roads were muddy but we arrived in good time and I accompanied the corps to Mr. Brights farm where she was buried in the orchard—came back to Brights to breakfast went to Church.

In October of the same year, Mr. Bright himself had a fatal accident which occurred, as witnesses at the inquest reported, when he was coming up McNabb's Hill with a load of potatoes. Another cart was descending the hill with a load of stones and when the horse turned towards Mr. Bright, he was pinned between the two carts. When William Helliwell arrived at the house that afternoon, he found Bright lying on a bed on the floor "Suffering most intensely" and although a doctor came and bled him "profusely", the next afternoon his agony was much worse. A few minutes before he died he sent for Helliwell who was waiting in the passage and demanded of him to "Burey me in Potters feild and take up my child at the farm and put her in the same hole, do you hear". After he died, William and his brother-in-law George Stegman walked to Potter's Field and chose a plot. At four o'clock the next day, the 18th of October, "the largest funeral that was ever in the City of Toronto" left the Bright house in the pouring rain. William was deeply moved by the occasion.

> The street was leterally filled for half a mile with carriages and waggons and Horses and the side walks were crouded to excess and at everey Street as the procession advanced it

William Helliwell's Diary, 1834.
Todmorden Mills Archives

was joined by large numbers and as we still advanced to the bottom of Yonge Street, the congregation of all churches joined.

It was such a solemn occasion that he added his own tribute in his diary:

> Such a Publick and General Expression of Regret was Never Seen in Toronto and well did he deserve it fore a better Husband kinder parent a more dutiful child or a sincere freind or a more charitable man is not to be found. I heard several say that he had not left another like him. It was dark when we arrived back High and low rich and was there all classes of society.

After the funeral, William helped his brothers-in-law, George Stegman and Thomas Bright, settle the estate. [25] The following month, William took Miss Nancy, Sally and Jane to Potter's Field to visit their father's grave and on the 22nd of November, there is a surprising entry in Helliwell's diary:

> This morning I road into Church and tooke dinner at Stegmans and attended the afternoon servis and after the servis was over Mrs. Bright got her baby christened William John myself and Mr. Atkinson sponsors and Mrs. Atkinson also.

Poor Mrs. Bright, a new baby and a dead husband all in one year. The funeral may have delayed the christening or the child may have been born after his father's accident.

Christmas that year was tinged with sadness and, perhaps to escape the understandable gloom of the Bright household, William took one of the girls on an outing. His description calls to mind the Bartlett prints portraying the Bay in winter, as well as the topographical landscapes painted by officers in the Garrison:

> I took Mrs. Helliwell down to her mothers in the light waggon and when I took him out of the waggon I put him into Wm. Brights slay and took Miss Jane riding onto the ice we took a direct coarse from the windmill for the Lighthous and continued on that coarse till we made the shore and then coasted along the island to the big House and then took another large turn around in the centre of the Bay and returned to dinner.

The Brights often visited the Helliwell's Don Valley home as well. The diary speaks of a "housefull" when "Master Charles and Misses Salley and Jane Bright and James Worts and his sister and Mr. and Mrs. Stegman and old Mrs. Stegman and Thomas all came". When visitors came, the families often went for walks in the valley. One day, William Helliwell took Caroline Bright up the hill as far as the Sinclairs' (which was near the Taylors') and this may have been the occasion when she met her future husband, George Taylor.

Nancy Bright, who later married George Taylor's oldest brother John, seems to have been a particular favourite of Helliwell. Throughout the years, he often spoke of her in his diaries. He remembered her birthdays and noted the events of her life such as the birth of her first child, and he commiserated when she fell and dislocated her shoulder. After dinner on

Christmas Day in 1837, he drove her up Yonge Street as far as Gallows Hill. They had much to talk about, for that morning they had all been to church where "the new Organ was plaid for the first time" and during the service the fire bell rang and

> a greater part of the congregation ran out of Church. It was a small house in the New Street verey little damage was done by the fire but the House was almost pulled to peas by the people.

In those days whenever there was a fire in York, volunteer fire wardens had the authority to conscript help, but it is obvious that such assistance had its limitations.

Unfortunately, the early diaries end in 1841 and are not extant again until 1879. The last diary notes that a fire destroyed many of Helliwell's papers. Because of this, we will never know why Elizabeth died in 1843, the year her sixth child was born. She and William had had four daughters and two sons, but their three-year old son, William Jr., died in an accident in the grist mill in 1844.

Elizabeth's sister, Jane Bright, was sent to help and to look after the children and it is not surprising that William married her in 1845. She was twenty-five and his junior by ten years. Jane proved to be much stronger than her sister Elizabeth and produced eleven children, lived a long life and died at eighty-three. One is tempted to say that it was a marriage of convenience except that Jane's first baby was born six and a half months after they were married. William always remembered his "Dear Girl"—his first wife—but he never once refers to Jane in later diary entries.

John Taylor's property was higher up the river than the Helliwells', close to where several streams converged to form the Forks of the Don. It was originally owned by Parshall Terry, who built a sawmill there about 1800. His widow, Rhoda, sold it to Major David Secord in about 1809 and then Samuel Sinclair bought it in 1817. [26] Sinclair was one of those minor background figures who had lived in the valley since 1797. He was a loyalist from New England who had first gone to New Brunswick before coming to Upper Canada. He joined the York Volunteers at the beginning of the War of 1812 and was wounded in General

Brock's expedition to Detroit. He married Anne Skinner, whose first husband had been killed during the war, and ran the Skinner mills on the upper Don for her until 1821. Sinclair was said to have owned property in Vaughan Township as well and it is possible that he was the one to persuade John Taylor to look for land in the Don Valley.

Immediately north of Taylor's new property lived William Lea and his family, after whom Leaside is named. The Leas' story was similar to that of the Taylors. They sailed from Liverpool in 1818 and after three months reached Pittsburgh, via Philadelphia. Because they were unhappy there, Lea decided to go alone to Upper Canada before moving his family again. He found the property he was looking for in the Don Valley and after buying 200 acres at a guinea an acre [27] he sent for his wife and son to join him. Later, William Lea Jr. described the journey with his mother along the shore of Lake Erie, across the Niagara River at Black Rock, and past the Falls, which he remembered hearing. The first thing that gave his mother courage was "seeing the British soldiers in their scarlet uniforms at Niagara in 1819". [28]

The Lea farm consisted of a small log house and a few cleared acres (Lot 13, Concession IIIFB) at the corner of the present Lea Avenue and Laird Drive. By 1828, the Leas had built the first brick house in the area. Lea described the Don Valley as he remembered it and it must have been a rural Eden:

> *The Don winds through a broad valley, the bottom lands immediately adjoining the river, which are usually flooded in the spring time, yielding rich pasturage. The banks which are thickly wooded rise abruptly, sometimes from the water, but more often at a considerable distance. They are broken by ravines, where tributary streams unite their waters with the Don, and occasionally these bluffs enclose a wide space, giving an amphitheatre-like effect. The river pursues a serpentine course, but the general direction in ascending it is northward for about four miles, when it takes a turn to the east the same characteristic being observable . . . The wildness and beauty of the ravines, glen, and stretches of woodland present attractions for the lover of nature not readily surpassed in this part of Canada.* [29]

William Lea, 1814-1893.
Todmorden Mills Archives

The history of the Lea family has been described elsewhere,[30] as has that of another neighbour, Phillippe de Grassie, who bought the east half of Lot 8, Concession IIIFB, in 1832. De Grassie was another new-comer to this part of the Valley, who bought in the summer after the Taylors had arrived, and two years later they owned adjoining properties. De Grassie was a tall, handsome officer of noble lineage, well-educated, but totally unsuited to pioneer life. Susanna Moodie could have been describing him when she wrote:

> ... a hand that has long held the sword and been accustomed to receive implicitly obedience from those under its control, is seldom adapted to wield the spade and guide the plough . . .[31]

Someone like Samuel Sinclair, who was illiterate, survived much better in this primitive environment than someone with such fine sensibilities and lack of judgement as De Grassie. Unlike the Helliwells, who had a long history of running a business in England, his lack of financial experience further added to his misery. His memoirs, written when he was an old man, reveal all the disillusionment and bitterness that so many of his class experienced when they came to the new world.[32]

He was born on the 15th of May, 1793 in Italy, the son of an Italian captain and an Austrian baron's daughter who was lady-in-waiting to the Queen of Naples. He received his education in France and served with the French army in Spain until he was taken prisoner and sent to England. There, he changed allegiance and joined the British, evidently a not uncommon practice in those days. After his last posting in the West Indies, he returned to England and went to live in Chichester. He married and to support his family and to supplement his income taught French, Spanish and Italian to the local gentry. In his memoirs, he wrote that he was on the point of receiving a professorship in Modern Languages at the Naval College at Portsmouth when he was persuaded to emigrate to Canada and take advantage of free land grants being offered to soldiers of the Crown. De Grassie admitted that, while his military years had been the happiest of his life, the debts he had incurred buying expensive uniforms continued to plague him. In addition, his family had increased in size and his "wife's sight was becoming worse every day." For these impractical reasons, he was enticed by the prospect of bettering himself in a new country and had visions of being one of the landed gentry, farming vast estates—an occupation for which he had no training whatsoever.

He sold his house and part of his furniture and sailed for Quebec with his wife and seven children in July of 1831 in a ship which he chartered from Southhampton. In addition to the £3,500 sterling, he brought letters of introduction and a collection of articles which he later found were "incongruous" for life in Canada. These included ploughs which were quite unsuitable, a portable flour mill, blacksmith's and carpenter's tools and, as a final touch, thirty-six cow bells and sixty sheep bells. One misfortune followed another, commencing with the near shipwreck of his chartered vessel in the Gulf of St. Lawrence before the family had even set foot in Canada. After stopping in Quebec and Montreal, the family finally arrived in York on September 29, 1831. Here, De Grassie wrote, "were to be blighted all my hopes of prosperity", and indeed the combination of unforseen circumstances and his own lack of experience led to disaster after disaster. His account of what happened to his family and himself is a heart-breaking story of misadventure and broken dreams.

The family spent its first winter at the Steamboat Hotel and De Grassie renewed his friendship with the Governor, Sir John Colborne. He was advised to take up land in the Talbot Settlement and set out to reach it by stagecoach. The roads were impassable because of the mud and, learning that he would have to walk the last seventy miles, he returned to York on foot. He was next offered thirty-six acres which in time became valuable since it was part of the Garrison Common, south of Queen Street, west of Bathurst Street. De Grassie declined it as not fitting to his station but later regretted the lost opportunity of making a profit.

He was obviously impatient to own land and in July of 1832 bought one hundred acres in the Don Valley (the east half of Lot 8, Concession III FB) for £525 from fellow Italians Franco Rossi and his wife. [33] He started at once to have the land cleared and a commodious frame house built. Eight months later, he received a Crown Grant for the east half of Lot 6, Concession III FB and the east half of Lot 7, Concession III FB, 200 acres which adjoined his property to the south. Unhappily, his good fortune was short lived. One month later, on April 14, 1833, a fire destroyed everything while he and his family were visiting in York. He described the tragedy in his memoirs:

> While the house was burning, some of my neighbours offered their services to save the furniture etc., but they kindly saved only the wine of which they freely partook and soon became so drunk as to be unable to be of any service. In this fire, I lost my furniture, clothing, complete silver dinner service, complete service of costly china and a supply of provisions for six months with money and jewelry.

By the 15th of April, he was in such dire straights that he was forced to sell his newly acquired Crown Grant for £700. He had built a sawmill on his original piece of land, which included a part of the Don River, and purchased two yokes of oxen and two spans of horses, but his situation did not improve. He even had a new saddle horse stolen from him and by 1834,

> Finding expenses heavy and being unable to carry on the saw mill, I rented it for £25 a year. Then another stroke of my old misfortune befell me and as misfortune seldom comes alone, to crown it all, the man to whom I had rented my mill ran away, leaving his rent unpaid. At this juncture, I heard a rumour that all half-pay officers were to be recalled into active service, and having a large family of young children and my affairs in such an unsettled state on account of the fire, I committed my half-pay although strongly advised not to do so by my sincere and good friend Sir J. Colborne who told me that if I did so, I would live to repent it. I had a short time before erected a stable for my horses, and having no other shelter in the wilderness, I was glad to live in the stable and one of my children was literally born in a stable and laid in a manger.

He must have used his new source of revenue to buy back his Crown Grant which he then promptly sold at a profit of £54. [34]

The purchaser, John C. Green, was probably helping him out, for within a year De Grassie bought it back for the same amount. [35]

In 1837, when the call came to defend Toronto against William Lyon Mackenzie, two of the residents of the Don Valley acted without hesitation. Phillippe De Grassie, as a retired officer, immediately saw his duty to the Crown and volunteered his services, and William Helliwell, as a Captain in the North York Militia under Colonel Duncan Cameron, assumed responsibility for weekly drills and rallies. One of the recruits among the hundred and eighty men under his command was Lieutenant Taylor, who is presumed to be John, the oldest of the three brothers who came to North America in 1821. For years the Taylor family had a sword in its possession which was supposed to have been the one he carried during the rebellion. Although the uprising merely amounted to a few skirmishes, a futile appeal to arms, the dispersal of the rebels and Mackenzie's flight to the United States, for De Grassie it was a bitter experience. His own words describe it best:

> *On the evening of the day that the rebellion broke out, as a well-wisher of law and order, I went to Toronto to offer my services to the Government, accompanied by my two daughters and narrowly escaped being taken prisoner by Matthews' troop which was going to Mr. Helliwell's place, where though uninvited guests, they regaled themselves. Having proceeded a little further I sent my daughter back and arrived in Toronto where I found nothing but excitement and confusion and went to the Government House. I was then Captain of the North York Militia, but as a volunteer joined the Scarboro Militia forces under the command of Colonel MacLean.*

He remained on duty at the Parliament Buildings for three days. His daughter Cornelia was an inadvertent heroine although her story is still unrecognized in the annals of the rebellion and should be included in the exploits of the residents of the Don Valley:

Parliament Buildings, Toronto, corner of King and Simcoe Streets.
Ontario Archives

During three days I was in the Parliament House, frequently visited by my family. I said that I would endeavour to ascertain the number of the rebels on Yonge Street. One of my daughters about thirteen years of age, accordingly who was a capital rider, rode out under the pretence of wishing to know the price of a sleigh, went to the wheelwright's shop close to Montgomery's Tavern, and being suspected was taken prisoner by some of the rebels who ordered her to dismount. To this she demurred and during the altercation with her captors MacKenzie came in with the news that the Western Mail was taken. Amidst the general excitement my little girl had the presence of mind to urge her horse and ride off at full speed amidst the discharge of musketry. A ball went through her saddle and another through her riding habit.

Arrived in Toronto she was taken before Sir F.B. Head, the Governor to whom she gave valuable information as to the numbers and condition of the rebels—thus the loyalists were encouraged, measures were taken to meet MacKenzie's attack and so my poor child was the means of saving Toronto where he had many partisans.

This exploit was also described in the October 6, 1838 issue of the New York *Albion,* which enlarges a little on De Grassie's account:

> . . . *[Cornelia De Grassie] reached the city bringing news of the robbery of the public mail and described the numbers of the rebels to be greatly exaggerated.*

The same article describes what happened to her sister Charlotte who

> . . . *had been detained by the loyal party at the market house, when one of the officers begged her to have the kindness to take a dispatch as they had no horsemen to send out. She complied with the request after which she set out on her return home in the evening. When near the corner of the bush before Sinclair's clearing a large party of rebels fired at her and wounded her . . .*

That same night

> *Cornelia arrived safely home . . . at about eleven o'clock having seen her father. She therefore crossed the bush again on Thursday morning and followed the loyal troops to Yonge Street. She was returning home to inform her mother of the events of the day and to give assurance of her father's safety when upon her arrival at the Don Bridge she discovered that Matthews had set it on fire. Instantly she returned to the city and gave the alarm. Then unable to pass the bridge on her pony in consequence of the great damage it had received, she left the animal in the city and proceeded on foot at eleven o'clock at night though the district was filled with dispersed rebels.*

No official acknowledgement of her services was ever made to Cornelia De Grassie. Her father particularly resented this oversight since she had provided invaluable information at her own peril.

William Helliwell's participation in the rebellion was far less dramatic:

> ... I walked into the City from the Don and on arriving at the Parliament found men assembling and preparing for a march to dislodge the insurgents ... On arriving there I immediately went into the building to procure a gun and equipment and having secured one was going out when I was met by Sir John Beverley Robinson... who stopped me and said he was in search of a reliable man to take charge of the powder magazine in the basement of the building ...

Later, he was sent to a plumber's shop where he made two pailfuls of musket balls—a necessary role but not conducive to heroism.

That winter of 1837 the weather was so severe that Susanna Moodie described it as a "year never to be forgotten in the annals of Canadian History". [36] De Grassie suffered so much from the cold and hardships which he endured when he was in command of a company under Colonel Baldwin that he attributed the loss of all his teeth to it. William Helliwell, too, complained of the intense cold when he and Lieutenant Taylor went to drill at Hogg's Hollow in January.

Unlike the Helliwells and Taylors, once the rebellion was over there is little left to say about the De Grassies. It is clear from the memoirs that Phillippe's experiences during the rebellion only added to his disillusionment and that he regretted his decision to leave England. He was the personification of what Mrs. Moodie described as:

> the large majority of emigrants who were officers of the army and navy who came with their families and were a class perfectly unfitted by their previous habits and standing in society for contending with the stern realities of emigrant life in the backwoods. [37]

The last 100 acres owned by De Grassie in the Don Valley were purchased by the Taylors in 1866 [38] and after this his family moved to Toronto and lived near the corner of Church and Carlton Streets. The 'e' at the end of the surname was eventually dropped, but posterity, in fact, was kind to Phillippe. In the Don Valley, local residents spoke of De Grassi Hill for many years and were familiar with De Grassi House, a small frame cottage on its west side. Although Phillippe claimed that his services in Upper Canada went unrecognized, a street just east of Broadview Avenue and north of Queen Street was named after the family. Furthermore, anyone who is familiar with Innisfil Township on Lake Simcoe will know De Grassi Point on the west side of Cook's Bay. While there are several theories as to the origin of the name, the most accepted one is that it was named after one of Phillippe's sons, Alfio, [39] who was active in municipal politics and in 1865 was a deputy for the Toronto Masonic District, which at that time included Simcoe County. *The Origins of the Names of Post Offices of Simcoe County* states that "the De Grassie family never lived at the place that now bears their name, but members of it, particularly Alfio, visited thereabouts for hunting and fishing".[40] One of John Taylor's grandsons, as a child, remembered seeing Phillippe De Grassi whom he described as a tall, dark man who commanded respect.[41] He died when he was eighty-one and was buried in St. James' Cemetery.

In the years immediately following the rebellion, life was uneventful for the residents of the Don Valley except for the exigencies of daily living common to all who lived in a rural environment. The Taylors farmed, built a saw and grist mill at the Forks of the Don, lumbered, and bought land. Whenever they could, they acquired more land, whether from Samuel Sinclair, William Lea, De Grassie or the Crown, until eventually they owned almost 4,000 acres.

Notes

1. (BR), William Helliwell, *Memorandums,* prepared from my father's writings, written by James Helliwell, unpublished, 1896.
2. E. Darke & I. Wheal, "Todmorden Mills: a 19th-Century Mill Town," p. 23.
3. *Ibid.,* p. 23.
4. E.C. Guillet, *Inns and Taverns* (Toronto: author, 1954), 2 vols., v. I, pp. 51, 55.
5. E. Darke & I. Wheal, p. 23.
6. William Helliwell, *Memorandums,* p. 10.

7. (Ontario Archives, hereafter, OA), *Canada Land Petitions,* 1827-1829, reference, TC 2836-1827-1836, Petition dated York, February 15, 1828.
8. John Ross Robertson, *Landmarks of Toronto* (Toronto: Toronto Evening Telegram, 1898), 6 vols., v. I, pp. 428 - 429.
9. *Ibid.*, p. 428 - 429.
10. *The Backwoods of Canada: 1836, Letters from the wife of an emigrant officer* (Toronto: Coles Publishing Co., reprinted, 1971), p. 181.
11. Family Papers of Dorothy Bright, unpublished, in the possession of the author.
12. *Ibid.*
13. *Ibid.*
14. Austin S. Thompson, *Spadina* (Toronto: Pagurian Press, 1975), p. 117.
15. (Anglican Diocesan Archives, Toronto) St. James' Cathedral, Marriage Register.
16. Edith Firth (ed.), *The Town of York: 1815 - 1834* (Toronto: University of Toronto Press, 1962), map of York, opposite p. 20.
17. R.O. #2605, #2567, #6222 and #6644.
18. J.E. Middleton, *Municipality of York, A History* (Toronto: The Dominion Publishing Co., 1923), 3 vols., v. 1, pp. 168 - 169.
19. Henry Scadding, *Toronto of Old,* edited by F.H. Armstrong (Toronto: Oxford University Press, 1966), p. 365.
20. Edith Firth (ed.) *The Town of York: 1815 - 1834,* p. 128.
21. Marriage Register, St. James Cathedral.
22. J. Lounsborough, *The Privileged Few* (Toronto: Art Gallery of Ontario, 1980), p. 28.
23. *Commemorative Biographical Record of the County of York* (Toronto: J.H. Beers Co., 1907), p. 317.
24. Edith Firth, p. 84. "Wragg and Co. was a large Montreal firm of ironmongers. In 1826, it opened a branch in York ... The York branch was managed by George B. Williard."

25. This was a tedious business according to the diaries and involved many trips to the city to see the authorities—Captain Fitzgibbon, whom Edith Firth says was the Assistant Adjutant-General, Dr. Powell, a lawyer and Justice of the Peace, who was one of the seconds in the famous Ridout-Jarvis duel in 1828, and John E. Small, Clerk of the Privy Council.
26. E. Darke & I. Wheal, p. 12.
27. J.I. Rempel, *The Town of Leaside: A Brief History* (Toronto: East York Historical Society, 1982), p. 3.
28. *History of the County of York*, v. II, p. 195.
29. *The Toronto Evening Telegram*, 4 February 1881, William Lea, paper read to the Canadian Institute.
30. See, J.I. Rempel, *The Town of Leaside, A Brief History*.
31. Susanna Moodie, *Roughing it in the Bush*, p. xviii.
32. (TMA), "Narrative of Captain Philippe de Grassie". Charles Sauriol, who published and edited *The Cardinal*, a Conservation Outdoor Magazine, donated his extensive research on the Don Valley, including the information on De Grassie, to the Todmorden Mills Archives.
33. R.O. #9126. See also, Patent, 7 March 1833.
34. R.O. #11248.
35. R.O. #12410.
36. Susanna Moodie, p. 391.
37. *Ibid.*, p. 4.
38. R.O. #69000.
39. D. Williams, *The Origins of the Names of Post Offices of Simcoe County* pp. 20-21.
40. *Ibid.*, pp. 20-21.
41. (TMA), John H. Taylor in conversation with Charles Sauriol.

The Daughters

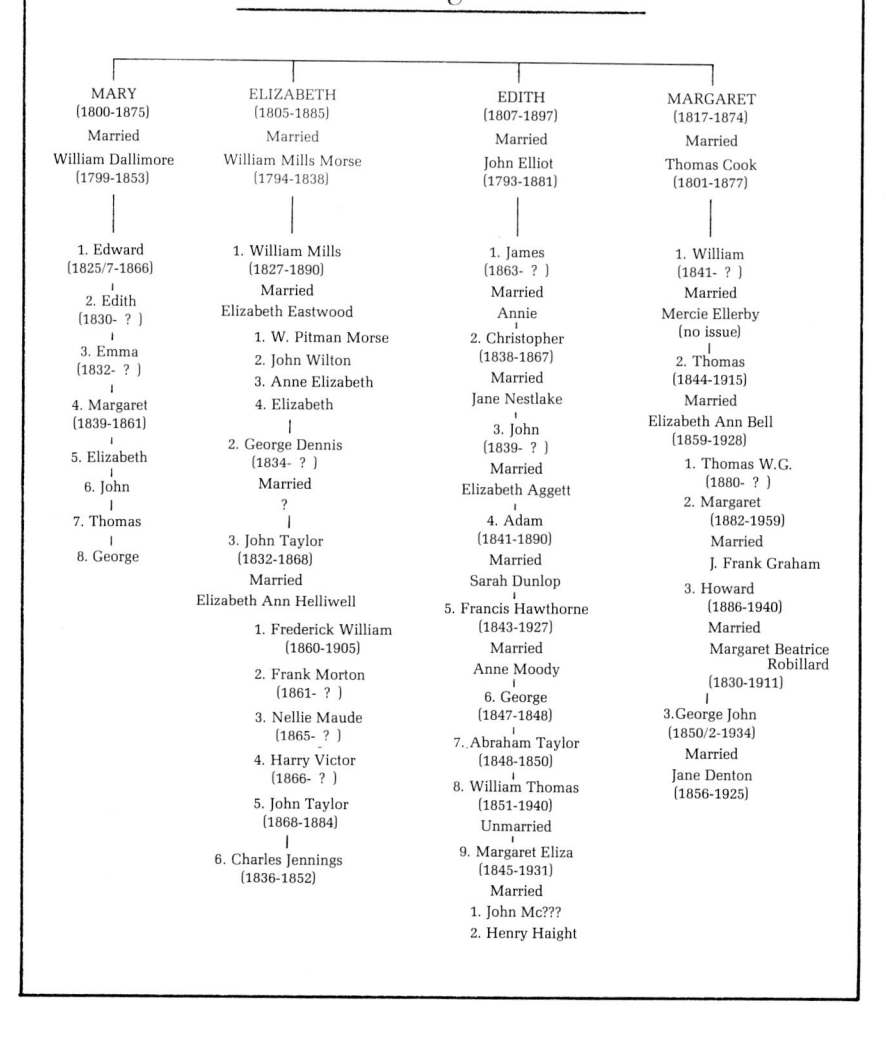

MARY	ELIZABETH	EDITH	MARGARET
(1800-1875)	(1805-1885)	(1807-1897)	(1817-1874)
Married	Married	Married	Married
William Dallimore	William Mills Morse	John Elliot	Thomas Cook
(1799-1853)	(1794-1838)	(1793-1881)	(1801-1877)

MARY — William Dallimore:
1. Edward (1825/7-1866)
2. Edith (1830- ?)
3. Emma (1832- ?)
4. Margaret (1839-1861)
5. Elizabeth
6. John
7. Thomas
8. George

ELIZABETH — William Mills Morse:
1. William Mills (1827-1890)
   Married Elizabeth Eastwood
   1. W. Pitman Morse
   2. John Wilton
   3. Anne Elizabeth
   4. Elizabeth
2. George Dennis (1834- ?)
   Married ?
3. John Taylor (1832-1868)
   Married Elizabeth Ann Helliwell
   1. Frederick William (1860-1905)
   2. Frank Morton (1861- ?)
   3. Nellie Maude (1865- ?)
   4. Harry Victor (1866- ?)
   5. John Taylor (1868-1884)
6. Charles Jennings (1836-1852)

EDITH — John Elliot:
1. James (1863- ?)
   Married Annie
2. Christopher (1838-1867)
   Married Jane Nestlake
3. John (1839- ?)
   Married Elizabeth Aggett
4. Adam (1841-1890)
   Married Sarah Dunlop
5. Francis Hawthorne (1843-1927)
   Married Anne Moody
6. George (1847-1848)
7. Abraham Taylor (1848-1850)
8. William Thomas (1851-1940) Unmarried
9. Margaret Eliza (1845-1931)
   Married
   1. John Mc???
   2. Henry Haight

MARGARET — Thomas Cook:
1. William (1841- ?)
   Married Mercie Ellerby (no issue)
2. Thomas (1844-1915)
   Married Elizabeth Ann Bell (1859-1928)
   1. Thomas W.G. (1880- ?)
   2. Margaret (1882-1959)
      Married J. Frank Graham
   3. Howard (1886-1940)
      Married Margaret Beatrice Robillard (1830-1911)
3. George John (1850/2-1934)
   Married Jane Denton (1856-1925)

54

III

THE DAUGHTERS

John Taylor's four daughters—Mary, Elizabeth, Edith and Margaret—are shadows in time, faceless figures who can be recognised only by the cemetery markers which bear their names. Women of their class and time lived within the confines of domesticity and very little is known about their lives. Although they lived within a broad family circle, which extended from Vaughan Township to the Don Valley and Pickering Township, their descendants have all but disappeared. Not even one picture of these women can be located. Their memory suffered the same fate as too many in past generations. One member of Margaret's family reported that "all those old pictures and Bibles went into the garbage long ago" [1] and none of the other sisters' relatives could be traced. In spite of this, what does come to light indicates that members of their families formed a large interwoven network whose names continue to appear from time to time.

I

Mary, the oldest sister, was twenty-one when she left England with her parents and she married William Dallimore. [2] Nine of their children have been recorded: Emma, Edith, Margaret, Mary, Sarah, John, Thomas, George and Henrietta. [3] In 1844, William Dallimore's name was associated with the three Taylor brothers on a document which indicated that his family was then living in the Don Valley. [4] He died in 1853 when he was fifty-four and Mary died in 1875 at the age of seventy-five.

As rural residents, they would have had little significance in the history of the area if it were not for their house and Donlands Farm where they lived. The house, which was a landmark until it burned down in 1940, was purchased by W.F. McLean in

The Dallimore House after it was renovated by W.F. McLean, photographed in 1922.
Toronto Telegram photograph collection, (photographer unknown), York University Archives

1914. He was the proprietor of the *Toronto World* and had been a Conservative Member of Parliament for York. He owned about nine hundred acres of land in the Don Valley, which included the Dallimore's old farm, part of the Taylor property north of Eglinton, and the Milne property where the woollen mill, another landmark of the upper Don, was located. [5] When he and his daughter Molly decided to live in the Dallimore house, she said that they "added just as much again to match the lovely work using field stone and getting old time masons to do the work". [6] A picture of the house was published in the *Toronto Telegram* on October 13, 1922. At that time, Mr. McLean had offered to sell the property to the city for a park. The Board of Control refused the offer because of the cost of one million dollars and the property's inaccessibility.

Donlands Farm (Lot 1, Concession III FB) consisted of ninety-five acres and it was deeded to Mary Dallimore by her brother George Taylor the year before she died. [7] This unusual gift poses the tantalizing question of why the Taylors felt obliged to give her this property when she was an old woman of seventy-four. It had been acquired in 1851 as a Crown grant which in itself was unusual because most of the Crown lands close to Toronto had been taken up by then. [8] The Taylors timbered it as part of their lumbering operation and it was also reported that some of the pine trees which they cut measured six feet across and yielded an incredible fourteen cords of wood each.

II

Mary's sister, Elizabeth, is another shadowy figure. We know nothing about her, very little about her husband, and only slightly more about her sons, three of whom achieved a certain measure of local prominence. Elizabeth may have lived with her family on the farm in Vaughan Township for a short time before she married William Mills Morse and went to live in Niagara-on-the-Lake. Here her first son, named after his father, was born in 1827. [9] Another son was born at Black Rock near Buffalo in 1832 [10] and by 1836, the family had moved to York where Elizabeth's husband served as Pathmaster. [11] This was an elected position set out by statute in the second session of the first Parliament of Upper Canada in 1793 and carried with it a certain amount of recognition. Pathmasters, or overseers, were selected by the ratepayers at the annual township meetings and received a small remuneration to supervise the maintenance of the roads. William Mills Morse died in Cleveland in 1838 and it was said that he was interested in lakeboats [12] which may explain why the family moved around the perimeter of the lakes.

After her husband's death, Elizabeth joined her family in the Don Valley and it was here that her sons were raised. One of them, Charles Jennings, died when he was sixteen and was buried with his father in the Taylor family cemetery. Two of his brothers, William Mills Morse Jr. and John Taylor Morse formed a partnership as flour-dealers and bought part of Lot 15, Concession III FB from their uncles in 1851. [13] They had a business office on Francis Street in Toronto. [14] William and John Morse each married local girls, both called Elizabeth, who were the daughters of John Eastwood and William Helliwell respectively. William Morse Jr. bought a farm on Yonge Street and served in the local Council and as a Deputy Reeve from 1859 to 1862. [15] He

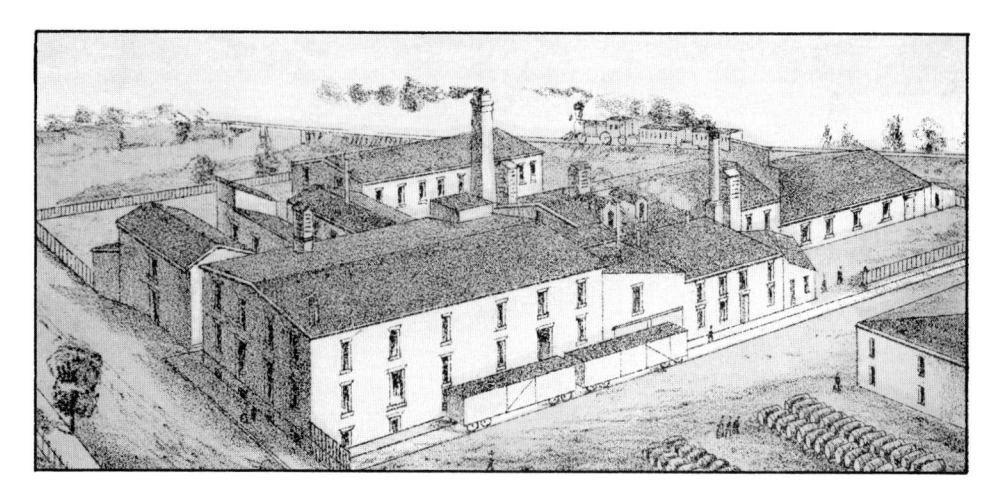

G.D. Morse & Co. Soap, Candle and Lard Oil Manufacturers.
Toronto Illustrated, Past and Present

later lived in Toronto at 111 College Street. [16] He was well regarded by the family and was named executor by his uncle, John Taylor. His name also appears as a witness on later Taylor documents. His brother John, who did not live very long, moved to Tollendale near Barrie, where he farmed and continued in the milling business. [17]

Their third surviving brother, George Dennis, had a varied career and even lived in Australia for seven years—the farthest that any of the Taylor relations ever travelled. When he returned home, he operated a distillery in Chippewa for two years and then in 1871 established his own business, the G.D. Morse Soap and Candle Works on River Street next to the Don station. Here he manufactured "no less than eight brands of laundry soap . . . every variety of toilet soap . . . and thousands of tallow candles" which he shipped all across the Dominion. [18] Both his house, "Crescent Place" at the corner of Wilton Crescent and South Park Street, and his factory on Front Street were of sufficient merit to be pictured in *Illustrated Toronto Past and Present*. [19] In 1878, he sold his business to Morrison and Taylor and operated a farm on Yonge Street although he lived at 186 Jarvis Street. [20]

Elizabeth Taylor Morse had at least nine grandchildren, some of whom moved to Manitoba, but like the Dallimores, her

Crescent Place, corner of Wilton Crescent and South Park Street, residence of G.D. Morse.
Toronto Illustrated, Past and Present

descendants cannot be traced. In the 1871 Census, she was listed as living with the family of her brother Thomas Taylor. It would seem that she was the one who looked after her father until he died in the 1860s and then, as was the custom, went to live with the family who needed her most. Thomas and Henrietta Taylor already had ten children and there were more to come. What better place could there have been for an elderly widowed aunt? There were so many children in those days and their early deaths were a constant source of grief: Elizabeth herself lost Charles Jennings when he was sixteen, her son John died when he was thirty-six and his son was drowned in Toronto Bay in 1884 when he too was sixteen.[21] She died the following year and was buried with her husband and son in the family cemetery.

III

Edith Taylor was the third sister and, perhaps because she was most responsible for the family when they came to Upper Canada, she did not marry until she was twenty-eight. She had looked after her father's household in Vaughan Township and when they first moved to the Don Valley. She had also been a mother to her sister Margaret who was only four when their mother died. Both Margaret and Edith married older men who had waited until they were established before they took on the responsibility of a family. Edith's husband was a forty-two year old farmer from Pickering Township called John Elliot, whom she married at St. James' Cathedral on August 19, 1835. Margaret married three years later, perhaps after her widowed sister Elizabeth Morse came to make her home with their father. Her husband was a successful miller from Vaughan Township. The sisters' lives were very different. Edith was a typical pioneer woman who lived on a farm in a log cabin where she raised eight of her nine children; [22] Margaret became the mistress of a handsome brick house with servants and had three sons. Edith was ninety when she died and outlived all her brothers and sisters while Margaret was the first of the family to die when she was fifty-four.

The little we know about Edith Taylor is based on a local history of Pickering Township. [23] It seems that her husband John Elliot, who was a shoemaker by trade, came to Canada with his brother William from Cumberland County in England in 1823 and purchased a farm near the 4th Concession in Pickering. He and his brother were listed among the first subscribers to the Scarborough Subscription Library, which was established in 1834, [24] and it cost them five shillings annually.

In 1825, the population of the township was only 830 and although many of the early hardships had passed, the roads were still poor, horses were scarce and John had to clear his own one hundred and fifty acre farm. The log cabin to which he brought Edith was a typical one with a large room downstairs with a fireplace at one end and perhaps two small bedrooms at the other. Upstairs, there was a large attic room lit by windows at the gable ends. [25] The Elliots had one daughter, Margaret Eliza, who was named after Edith's sisters, and seven sons: Christopher, James, John Adam, Francis Hawthorne, George, Abraham Taylor and William Thomas. As time went on and with seven sons to help, the work on the farm became easier. Their son Christopher went to school until he was fifteen and then worked on his father's farm until he and his brother John went into business buying and selling livestock.

Christopher had a serious accident when he was coming home from visiting his Taylor cousins:

Elliott Log Cabin, Concession III, Pickering Township
William McKay

It was in the depth of winter and he was driving a spirited horse hitched to a light sleigh or cutter. While crossing a bridge over the Don River on the outskirts of Toronto, a barking dog ran out and frightened the horse. The horse became fractious, overturned the sleigh and he was thrown from a bridge to the ice below striking the side of his head. A severe concussion of the brain resulted and he was taken to the home of one of his Taylor uncles who lived near the Don and there he hovered between life and death for some time. [26]

Christopher survived the accident and became a farmer near Uxbridge, but the rest of Edith's family have slipped into oblivion. "Elliot" became "Elliott" in time and there may still be families living in the Pickering area who are related to them. Their mother would have remained anonymous if it were not for the last diary of William Helliwell who, by coincidence, moved to Pickering Township. It was there that he lived for most of his life.

The move occurred after a disastrous fire on the night of January 10, 1847 destroyed a good part of the Helliwell brothers' settlement at the foot of Pottery Road hill. They lost most of the brewery, the distillery, the grist mill and Joseph's house; the total damage was estimated at $16,000 of which only $1,000 was recovered by insurance. Joseph stayed and rebuilt the grist mill which he operated until 1858, but William moved to property that his father had bought in 1820 at Highland Creek. [27] A graphic account of the fire was written in her diary by Joseph's wife Sarah:

> ... *the alarm of fire was Given Just as we were retiring to bed part of my family was already in bed also our men who slept in the top story of the house at the thrilling cry of Fire my dear Joseph and myself pushed to the door when to our utter astonishment and dismay the Coolers from which there was a communication to our house was all on Fire I felt conscious our dwelling house could not be saved and so it proved for I believe in less than two hours the brewery, dwelling house and Grist Mill were all consumed the loss of which can scarcely be estimated as it is not only the loss of property but has caused a complete stagnation of business ...*

Such a calamity strained even her devotion, but in humble fashion she wrote that it was her duty to accept what she felt was God's judgement:

> ... *the infinitely wise God my heavenly Father has been pleased to permit a heavy gloom to shade the sun of prosperity ...* [28]

William Helliwell was thirty-six when he, Jane and the children moved to Pickering and they prospered. There were seventeen children in all (from William's two marriages) and they lived in a house on the south side of the Kingston Road near the Highland Creek bridge. [29] There was a dam on the property originally constructed by William Cornell, an earlier resident, and here Helliwell built his new grist mill. In addition, he ran for public office when the Township Council was started in 1850 and served as a member for twelve years. He was also appointed a Justice of the Peace and, later, Commissioner of Fisheries for York County. Always enterprising, in 1865 he started the

Scarborough Hotel, Old Danforth Road
Courtesy of Prof. James Guillet

Commercial Hotel which for many years was a stopping place for the stage coaches travelling along the Kingston Road. [30] It had a long history, becoming Maxwell's Hotel and, later, the Scarborough Valley Hotel, before it burned down in 1938. Helliwell was not so successful with the Scarborough Oil Company, a rather questionable venture which was launched with the hope of finding oil in the Township. [31]

On April 14, 1879, there was a second disastrous fire for the Helliwells and in it William lost his papers, books and memorandums. He was sixty-eight at the time and after the fire devoted the rest of his life to farming. The subsequent journals are confined to calendar entries recording the weather, visits of relatives and friends, brief outings, the occasional wedding and frequent funerals. However, it is apparent that he never lost touch with the Taylors and particularly with Edith and her husband, who lived nearby. He describes John Elliot as an "old friend" whom he persuaded to buy shares in the ill-fated oil company. Also, George Taylor and his family stopped at the Helliwell's frequently when they came to Pickering to call on Edith. In September 1882, for instance, they arrived when he was "drawing corn" and "took dinner and tea" and another time they all attended Scarborough fair together. In addition, when Helliwell's duties as Commissioner of Fisheries took him to Toronto, he often stayed at "Beechwood", George Taylor's house and spoke of taking him "tracking along the river". One

63

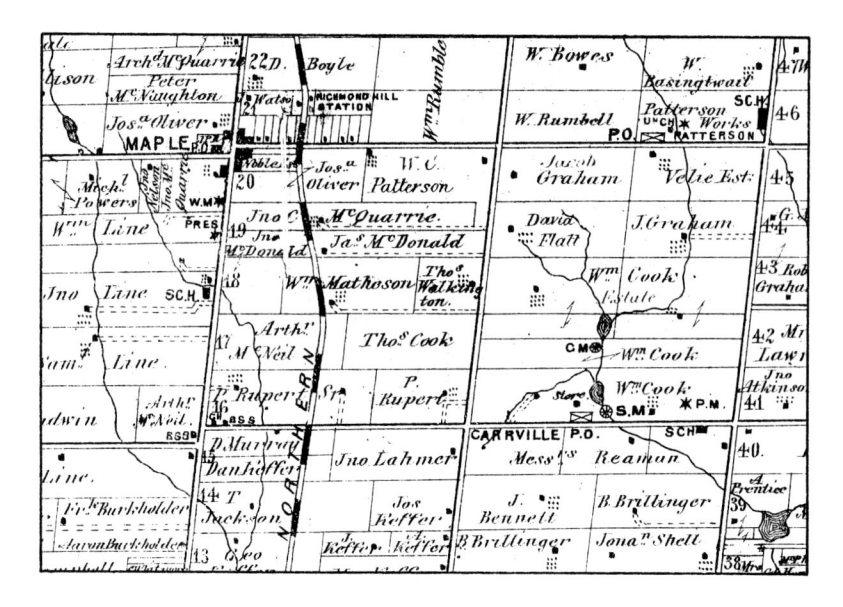

Vaughan Township, showing Thomas and William Cook's property.
Historical Atlas of York County, Miles and Company, 1878.

can almost see the two old men with their white beards searching for poachers' nests and hoping to find something illegal.

When George Taylor's brother Thomas died, Helliwell stayed over night for the funeral. He was also well acquainted with Thomas's in-laws, the Jobbitts, who lived on the next farm to his in Pickering (Lot 6, Concession 1). When news came that Mrs. Jobbitt had died in March 1884, he went to view her "corps" before her daughter Henrietta took it to her house in Todmorden "to be buried from thence". Both Mr. and Mrs. Jobbitt were buried in the Taylor cemetery and before the service Helliwell noted in his diary that he "slept at George Taylor's went to the city returned with James G. Worts [his brother-in-law] to the funeral".

William Helliwell lived long enough to serve on one of Scarborough's Centennial committees in 1896, but he died the following year at the age of eighty-six. [32] Edith Elliot died that same year and she and her husband are buried in the cemetery of St. George's Anglican Church in Pickering. Jane Helliwell, who had raised so many children, died in 1903 at the age of eighty-three.

IV

The marriage of John Taylor's youngest daughter, Margaret, to Thomas Cook was a good match, although she was only twenty and he was thirty-four. He was a successful miller-farmer who had been living in Vaughan Township since 1831. Along with his brother William, he owned 400 acres of land and two mills on a tributary of the Don River. [33] The grist mill had been built in 1816 and is thought to be the first in the township. The saw mill was erected by the Cooks in 1838. [34]

When Thomas Cook purchased this property in 1831, it consisted of Lots 17 and 18, Concession II and was called the Fisher Estate because it had been settled by Jacob Fisher, one of the German settlers from Berlin, Pennsylvania who had come to Vaughan in 1806. Fisher's son Michael inherited the property but decided to sell it and move to Huron County near Goderich, where he purchased several thousand acres. When his neighbours to the north, Edward and Mary O'Brien, heard that the land was for sale, they considered buying it themselves and dividing it with Mary's brother, Dr. Anthony Gapper. [35] They eventually moved to Shanty Bay on Lake Simcoe instead, but at the time Mary wrote in her diary that the property was of "considerable interest". [36] The O'Briens were also anxious to know who their new neighbours would be, for they depended on the owner of this land for the upkeep of their "best road". [37] In 1834, Thomas divided the property with his brother William [38] and together they farmed and operated the two mills that already had a monopoly on trade in that part of the township.

Thomas was the first of the brothers to marry and may have met Margaret Taylor through her family's former association with Vaughan, or because her brothers were also millers on the same river to the south-east. After the wedding, Thomas and Margaret Cook lived in the old Fisher house, but when their first son William was born, they moved to a mud-brick house that they built on Lot 16 bordering the Carrville Road. [39] Thomas Cook had been fortunate to receive a Crown Grant for this land which increased the holdings to 600 acres. [40] At this time, his brother William decided to rent his land to Nathaniel Kirby and returned to England where he married and had six children before coming back to Canada eighteen years later. [41]

	1844 Paddy Murphey Dr	Cr	108

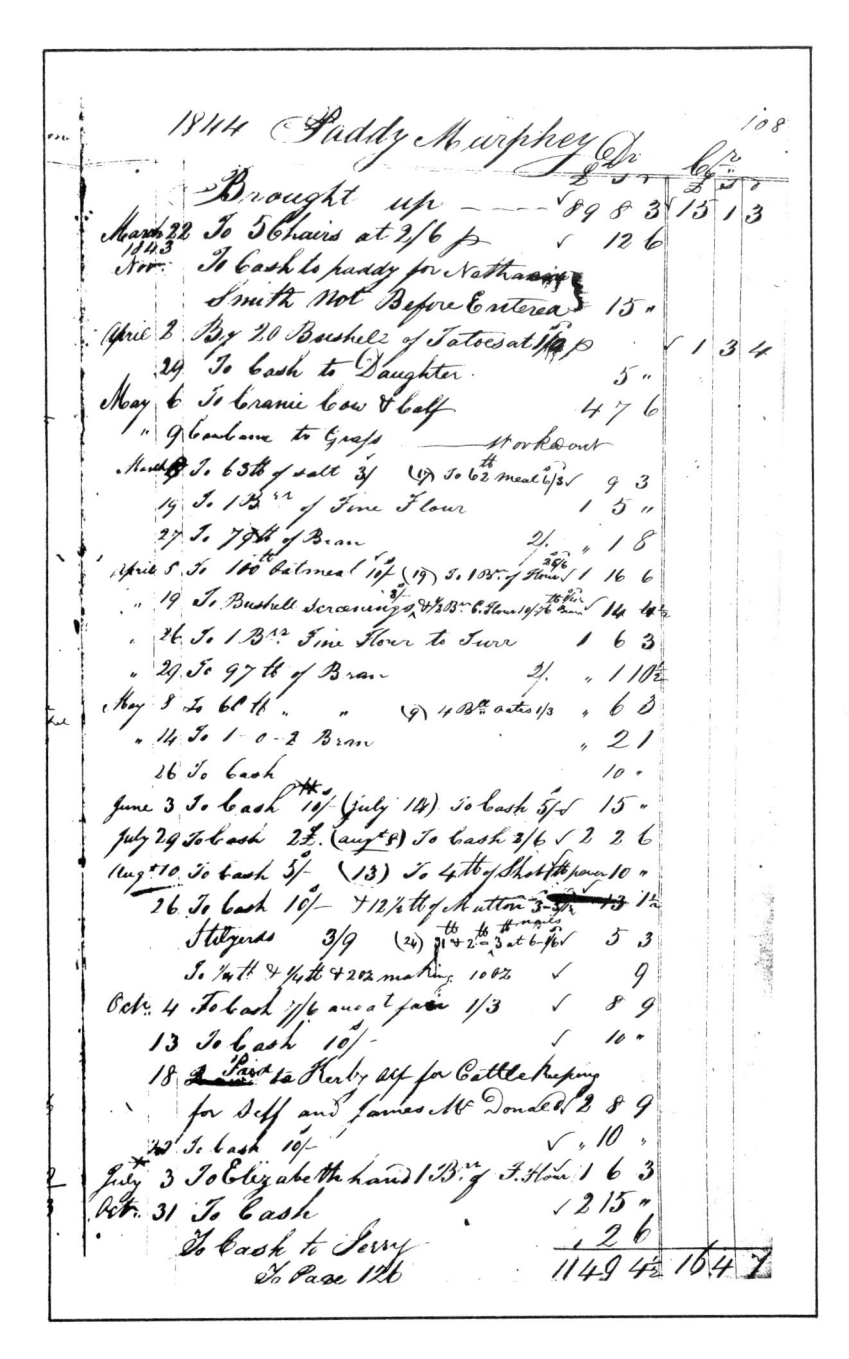

```
                                          £  s  d    £  s  d
               Brought up ———    89  3   15  1  3
March 22  To 5 Chairs at 2/6 p        12  6
1843
Nov       To Cash to paddy for Nathan
          Smith Not Before Entered    15  "
April 2   By 20 Bushels of Tatoes at 1/4 p        1  3  4
    29    To Cash to Daughter          5  "
May  6    To Cranie Cow & Calf         4  7  6
    "  9  Cow bare to Grass    Workd out
March 8   To 63 lb of Salt 3/  (9) To 62 meal 1/3   9  3
    19    To 1 B.r of Fine Flour       1  5  "
    27    To 79 lb of Bran     2/     "  1  8
April 5   To 160 lb Oatmeal 10/  (19) To 185 lb of Flour 1 16  6
    " 19  To Bushell Screenings &c &c C. Flour       14  4½
    26    To 1 B.12 Fine Flour to Turr  1  6  3
    " 29  To 97 lb of Bran       2/   "  1 10½
May  8    To 60 lb  "  "   (9) 4 Bh oates 1/3   6  3
    " 14  To 1-0-2 Bran                 "  2  1
    26    To Cash                       10  "
June 3    To Cash 10/ (July 14) To Cash 5/   15  "
July 29   To Cash 2/ (aug 8) To Cash 2/6     2  2  6
Aug 10    To Cash 5/   (13) To 4 lb of Shot pair 10 "
    16    To Cash 10/ + 12½ lb of Mutton 3-9½    13  1½
          Stilyards  3/9  (24) 21 + 2- 3 at 6 p.r    5  3
          To ¼ lb & ¼ lb & 2 oz making 10 oz   "  9
Oct. 4    To Cash 7/6 meal pan 1/3           8  9
    13    To Cash 10/-                  10  "
    18    Paid to Kerby self for Cattle keeping
          for self and James McDonald   2  8  9
    23    To Cash 10/-                 " 10  "
July 3    To Elizabeth Laird 1 B.r of F. Flour  1  6  3
Oct. 31   To Cash                       2 15  "
          To Cash to Jerry                 2  6
          To Page 126                 11 9  4½   16  4  7
```

An Account of Expenses of Jacob Baker

1859		To Cash to W.D. Bacon for Barker's Chattel Mortgage, Postage & Regist	5.50	
		To Cash to Sheriff for destraining and selling goods	28.60	
Septr	21	To Cash to Chas Pettys at St Thomas	218.67	
	22	To Cash to Lawyer at St Thomas for Registering	1.50	
Septr 1860	20	To Thos Cook expenses to Baker's home	11.20	
Septr		To Thos Cook expenses from Hamilton to Bakers and home again	7.40	
1860 April		To Wm Cook Jun expenses and paid to the Lawyer & Bailiff	31.22	
1860 July	24	To Cash Remitted to Chas Pettys and by T. Cook and acknowledged same	100.00	
Septr	12	To Cash sent by Wm Cook to Pettys	100.00	
"	28	" Cash paid by Wm Cook to Pettys out of Rent of $140.	77.00	
		To Cash paid by Wm Cook to Mark W. Cook paid on some Hundy for journeys in renting land and recd same of T. Cook	5.00	
Septr	28	By Rent and 77.00 ool cts paid to Pettys and	60.00	140.00
1859	"	By Proceeds of Sale		604.30
1861 Septr	1	By Rent to W. Cook paid Pettys 163.00 ool	163.00	235.00
		out of Rent and By Repairs of Barn 28.25 ool cts 28.25 and W. Logan paid Pettys ool cts on 12 March/62 . 43.75	43.75	
1862 Feby	22	To Cash Remitted to Pettys by T. Cook	102.00	
Septr	1	By Rent		235.00
Octob 1861	21	To Cash paid by W. Logan to Pettys Dol 100ct 100		
		To Cash W. Cook paid Pettys and Recd same out of Rent	$118.50 118.50	

Carrville Mill, built by Michael Fisher, Sr. in 1826, destroyed by fire in 1933.
Courtesy of George C.H. Snider

Business at the mills was so successful that Thomas Cook started a store in a small building near the grist mill and in 1844 moved it to a larger building near the Carrville Road. [42] A succession of storekeepers looked after it for him and after his death it served the community for over seventy years before it was eventually turned into a private house. The store and mills were the centre of activity for a large area which extended to the nearby villages of Thornhill, Richmond Hill, King, Hogg's Hollow and as far as Markham and York. The Cooks had two servants and a store clerk, Thomas Scholfield, who lived with them according to the Census of 1851. One of Thomas Cook's Day Books is still in existence [43] and is a meticulous record of both his affairs and the transactions at the store. Entries were made by Thomas and others, the spelling was occasionally phonetic, and the currency cited varied from sterling to dollars.

It is apparent that he had a number of employees including millers, labourers, and men to do repairs and farm work. One of the first was William Miller, who began work in November of 1836 at $24 per month, but the following June Cook mistakenly sold him three and a half gallons of whisky and, it was reported in the book, Miller "got drunk" and "left mill" having broken an iron saw for which he was charged 2/6. The rates paid then seem incredibly low but are indicative of the value of money. A labourer received $9 per month and Nathaniel Burr earned 5 shillings per day for farm work with his threshing machine. "Craidling and racking and binding" cost Cook 15 shillings; James Dodd, pump-maker, cleaned a well for £1, and it cost 2/6 to have pork-barrels repaired. Christopher Scanlin, a sawyer, came to work for Cook at the mill in 1849 and was paid $11 per month, but it was not a happy association, for in October of that year Scanlin "let the water run over the dam and break it" which was "wilfully done" and the "bull wheel was broken as well". Cook first rented the mill to George Squires for $25 a month in 1846 and a Mr. Hay was the first in a succession of store-keepers for his store. [44]

Accounts were held with Cook by such well-known Vaughan residents as Miles Langstaff, Hiram Dexter, Thomas Scholfield, Raymond Burr, Edward O'Brien and his mother-in-law, Mrs. Gapper, John Atkinson, William Keefer, Thomas Bone, Josiah Raymond (Reaman), and William Mellish. They were farmers and tradesmen who represented a variety of pioneer skills, including chopper, cooper, wheelwright, shingle-maker, shoe-maker, weaver, pumpmaker, wharfmaker, and chairmaker. Thomas Helliwell from York (whose brother William was the Taylor brother-in-law) patronised the mills from 1832 until 1842 and Margaret's brother, Thomas Taylor, purchased a "fat cow" for £5 in 1846. Cook himself bought cattle from William Morse, his wife's nephew, for £18/11/5 in 1851. The mills and store carried on a lively trade. Grain was ground into flour, wood was cut and sold for general construction, or made into flooring, shingles, lathes, barn boards and siding. All types of hardware were made, including nails, "inges", hay knives and stovepipes. The store even sold a feather bed and pillows, shoes were made by a shoemaker and a chairmaker charged Cook 5 shillings per chair. Whisky was also a common item of trade. It was bought from distillers in Markham and Hogg's Hollow and resold by the gallon or quart when the farmers came in for their regular

Cook family house, north-west of the Carrville United Church, Carrville Road, Vaughan Township.
Author's collection

Carrville United Church, Carrville Road, Vaughan Township.
Author's collection

supplies. Accounts were settled by various means—occasionally, there was payment in labour as when James Bertram paid his bill of £59/32/2 at the mill by working on Thomas Cook's mud-brick house, plastering the walls for two years after they moved in, installing stovepipes, and repairing and patching the brick oven. Sometimes the accounts were disputed and if payment was not forthcoming, Cook took his customers to court in Richmond Hill.

When he ran for Councillor in the first election in 1850, he was defeated. At this time Vaughan Township was divided into five wards and each ward elected a Councillor. They in turn elected a Reeve and Deputy Reeve for the township. Voting was done by open ballot with each man standing in front of the recording officer and publically announcing his preference. The vote was recorded and, in addition, motions were made proposing each man and a show of hands was counted. Cook ran against David Smellie in Ward I and when the show of hands favoured Smellie, Cook demanded that a poll be taken. However, this disappointment was superseded when he ran again two years later and was elected for the first of five successive terms. [45]

It is apparent from the Day Book that Cook often acted as a banker, lending money at interest and taking care of quite complicated transactions for his customers. His records pertaining to Jacob Baker illustrate his financial role in the community. He and Baker were old friends, dating from the days when he had built a new sawmill and Baker had designed and patented an overshot wheel eighteen feet in diameter for him. [46] From 1859 to 1863, Cook looked after Baker's affairs and earned the considerable sum of $1,200 for his expertise in legal matters. He paid mortgages, dealt with lawyers, bailliffs and sheriffs, and obtained the opinion of counsel; he rented Baker's property, looked after repairs to his buildings and travelled to St. Thomas and Hamilton on his behalf. Cook was obviously very competent, but unfortunately there is no explanation why Baker needed his services. Cook also looked after the affairs of Thomas and William Scholfield. He paid their taxes in Barrie, lent them £3 to buy a boat, and even paid one woman to do their washing and another to make shirts for them. Cook also acted as an agent for individuals; witness the account of Hiram Dexter: "In security for his sum I hold a power of turney for £100 and likewise for collecting rents of Robert Smith for the turn of 5 years".

Not all his customers were able to pay their bills and Cook hoped to recover a balance of £7/11/9 owed by Miles Langstaff in bankruptcy court. Patrick Murphy, who worked for him from time to time, ran up a large bill of £136/1/5. Cook called in John Nelson, a surveyor, who certified that he had measured four parcels of land belonging to Murphy that were to be transferred to Cook in lieu of payment, but, alas, the account was "lost by land being sold for taxes". It is not surprising that Cook was appointed a Justice of the Peace and "discharged his duties with much discrimination and judgement". [47]

In Vaughan Township, as elsewhere, the condition of the roads was a real problem in the nineteenth century. In the spring and summer, the mud and dust made travel difficult and unpleasant. Upkeep of the roads was the responsibility of each landowner and in 1842 Cook noted that he had paid James Hart £3 for road repairs. Wood was used to surface roads by the middle of the century and the Vaughan and King Plank Road Company purchased its supplies from Cook's mill. This company was responsible for the section of road that ran from the King boundry through Kleinberg, Pine Grove and Woodbridge. In one instance, it also purchased nails for the Troyer Hill road and lumber for a toll-house. The system of paying tolls was not popular with the farmers because the roads were generally in poor condition, but it was not until 1896 that tolls were abolished and the roads became a municipal responsibility.

The Day Book also deals with local education, which was an important aspect of rural life in Vaughan. Cook was the father of three sons and when the Carrville School was built by Nathaniel Burr in 1846, his five-year-old son, William, was enrolled as the youngest pupil. [48] Cook provided the wood for the shingles for the school. The actual shingles were made by a man named "Rhian" from Richmond Hill and it was duly noted that they were "verrey bad". Previously, classes had been held in whatever building was available. It was customary for parents to pay the teacher an amount per pupil and Cook noted that he had collected money on the teacher's behalf, including 10 shillings from a fellow miller, John Atkinson. The Canada West school system came into effect in 1850 and established a tax on real property to cover the costs. In 1852, Cook noted that he had collected £3/10/0, which included the school tax and tuition, from John Bennett.

The school was a welcome addition to the little community that had grown up around Cook's mills and store, located between Lots 15 and 16 on what is now the Carrville Road running east of Bathurst Street and south of Richmond Hill. At some time, it was called the village of Carrville, although why it was so named has never been determined. [49] A frame church was located farther to the east, but in 1857 Thomas Cook magnanimously decided to build a brick chapel on his property for the Methodist community. It was a major undertaking because he not only gave the land, [50] but he also paid for the materials and labour. From the first day in the spring when Harry Potter dug the foundation and Thomas Bone set in the foundation stones, it was a hive of activity. Ten men in all, including Thomas Cook's eldest son William (then a boy of fifteen), worked on the building. It was all meticulously recorded in the Day Book, from the 123 barrels of lime to the horse and cart that he hired. The wood was reported as the best, "all clear and good stuff", and the quantities and prices were listed for the "gysts" in the floor and roof, the timber for the walls, the wood for the pews and pulpit and the supplies for the windows and doors.

The first collection was taken up on July 12, 1857 and yielded £8/10/0. In addition, a few others donated £50 to the cause and Cook himself gave another £200 beyond the £378/7/17 which he had spent on the construction of the building. Fund-raising is endemic to all churches and another half page of the Day Book, dated 1861, is taken up with receipts. Thomas Dudley, Mr. and Mrs. Baldwin, Thomas Badger, N. Kerby and Thomas Bell were particularly generous over a six month period. A tea meeting at the Combs also raised £15/5/0. Cook even pencilled in the margin that Thomas Dudley had paid him for the deed and memorial of the land. It cost 37½ cents.

The Day Book was continued by Cook's son Thomas, but after his death the entries deteriorate and are largely written in pencil and crossed out after payment was settled. The transactions were for small amounts and it is obvious that business had declined. Young Henry Fisher was even allowed to write a poem in the book on September 4, 1883:

Cook family monument,
Carrville United Church
Cemetery.
Author's collection

When the golden sun is setting
And your mind from care is free
When of distant ones your thinking
Then dear Miller think of me.

    The story of Thomas Cook, the miller-farmer of Vaughan is in part a digression from the story of the Taylor family, but it is relevant for two reasons. The Taylors had lived for seven years in the next concession to the northwest of the Cook property and therefore would have been familiar with many of Cook's associates and customers. Secondly, it provides something of the milieu in which the youngest Taylor daughter lived. When Margaret Taylor Cook died at the age of fifty-four in 1874, her husband erected a handsome monument in the cemetery to the east of his church and dedicated it to his "beloved wife". He died three years later on Christmas Day when he was seventy-four and his sons buried him with his wife.

If the ghosts of Thomas and Margaret Cook were tempted to leave the cemetery on All Hallow's Eve, they would see little that they recognized. The village of Carrville has blended into the landscape except for the church which is still an active tribute to its founder. The barns have long disappeared and only the mill pond and a flume with the old millstone remain as reminders of their once thriving business. The old Fisher house and Cook's mud-brick house have been renovated and changed by various owners, and the store has been converted into a house. The most interesting house of all is still standing. At some unknown time, Thomas built an imposing Georgian brick house which is reached by a lane from the Carrville Road just west of the church. It is typical of the style, with a handsome square doorway, an observatory platform on the roof and originally it had a large verandah. It is situated so that Thomas Cook could live comfortably aloof from his enterprises, but still be within easy travelling distance of his operations and be able to see the church to the east. His son Thomas Jr. raised a family of five children there after his father's death, but since his occupancy the house has been sold several times.

Some of the Cook descendants still live in the area, but, little connection exists with their past; some time in the late 1880s, the sawmill closed because the supply of local timber disappeared. The grist mill was operated by a series of millers until it was destroyed by fire on November 16, 1953, [50] and the last of the original Cook farms was sold in 1959. [51]

Notes

1. Conversation with Mrs. Clarence Graham, a Cook descendant.
2. Taylor family cemetery. Other spellings include Dillamore, Dellamore, Dallimore and Delamore, but Dallimore is used in the cemetery.
3. Emma and Edith were baptized and confirmed at St. John's Anglican Church, York Mills. Margaret died in 1861 and is buried with her parents. The rest were recorded in the 1871 Census as living with their widowed mother. Edward Dalli-

more and his wife Sarah were buried in the Don Mills United Church cemetery, next to the Taylor family cemetery.
4. (TMA), Articles of Co-Partnership, Don Mills Road Company, 15 May, 1844. File X973.103.A-G.
5. P.W. Hart, *Pioneering in North York* (Toronto: General Publishing Co., Ltd., 1968), p. 237.
6. (TMA), Charles Sauriol, "The Story of the Don" (n.p., n.d.) File X973.344), p. 110.
7. R.O. #7436, East half, Lot I, Concession IIIFB.
8. Crown Patent, 17 June 1851.
9. *Commemorative Biographical Record of the County of York* (Toronto: J.H. Beers Co., 1907), p. 578.
10. *Ibid.,* p. 578.
11. *Historical Atlas for York County* (Toronto: Miles & Co., 1878), p. 10.
11. *The Commemorative Biographical Record,* p. 578.
13. R.O. #70563.
14. *The Commemorative Biographical Record,* p. 87.
15. *Ibid.,* p. 578.
16. P.W. Hart, p. 290.
17. *The Commemorative Biographical Record,* p. 578.
18. J. Temperlake, *Illustrated Toronto, Past and Present* (Toronto: Peter A. Gross, 1877), p. 283.
19. *Ibid.,* p. 378, plates, 24 and 23.
20. *Toronto Directory,* 1887, p. 719.
21. Taylor Family Cemetery; Diary of William Helliwell, 1884.
22. D. Boyle, *Township of Scarborough,* (Toronto: Wm. Briggs, 1896), appendix c, 150 acres.
23. William A. McKay, *The Pickering Story* (Township of Pickering Historical Society, 1961), p. 209.
24. W.R. Wood, *Past Years in Pickering Township* (Toronto: Wm. Briggs, 1911), p. 25.
25. W.A. McKay, p. 45.
25. *Ibid.,* p. 209.
27. *History of the County of York* (Toronto: E. Blackett Robinson, 1885), 2 vols., v. II, p. 270; Lots 7 and 8, Concession I.

28. (TMA), Diary of Sarah Helliwell, Jan. 1 - Mar. 14, 1847.
29. R.R. Bonis, *A History of Scarborough* (Scarborough Public Library, 1965), p. 68.
30. Scarborough Community Guide (*Mirror* Newspaper, n.d.), p. 11.
31. (TMA), James Helliwell, Notes on His Father's Diaries, 9th March, 1936.
32. R.R. Bonis, p. 106.
33. R.O. #8004, 1831, Lots 17 and 18, Concession II, Vaughan.
34. *History of the County of York,* v. II, p. 336.
35. (OA), O'Brien Journals, 1828-1838, ms 199, August 27, 1830. Or failing this, they thought of asking the Director of the Canada Company to buy the land and let Edward farm it.
36. *Ibid.*
37. *Ibid.*
38. R.O. #11098.
39. (RHPL), Memoirs of Jonathan Baker, unpublished, 1896, scrapbook #1, p. 80.
40. Crown Grant, 3 January, 1842.
41. According to Vaughan Township historian Mrs. Helen Schwabb, in conversation with the author.
42. Memoirs of Jonathan Baker, p. 81.
43. In the possession of the author.
44. G.E. Reaman, *A History of Vaughan Township* (Toronto: Vaughan Township Historical Society, 1969), p. 100.
45. *Ibid.,* p. 67.
46. Memoirs of Jonathan Baker, p. 86.
47. *History of the County of York,* p. 336.
48. G.E. Reaman, p. 169.
49. *Ibid.,* p. 133.
50. *Ibid.,* p. 100.
51. *Ibid.,* p. 194.

Taylor Brothers – The Grandsons

JOHN HAWTHORNE
(1853-1940)
Married
Mary Matilda McLean
(1859-1930)

1. John
   Married
   Delie Thomas
2. Charles McLean
3. Morton
   Married
   Marie Morgan
4. Jessica Victoria
   (1866-1977)
5. Stuart
   Married
   Helen
6. Dorothy
   Married
   Ben Langley
7. Harold A.
8. Walter
   Married
   Marie Cringan
9. Edith
10. Audrey

THOMAS BRIGHT
'White Tom'
(1857-1903)
Married
Henrietta Victoria Davies
(1857-1944)

1. Edith May
   (1881-1885)
2. Etta Florence
   (1883-1977)
   Married
   George Gale
   (1913-1982)
3. Frank
   (1884-1885)
4. Norman Thomas
   (1886-1891)
5. Fidelia Evelyn
   (1888-1965)
   Married
   Harry Hayburn Miller
   (1886-1964)

JOHN FREDERICK
Married
Elizabeth 'Lizzie' Patterson

1. Kate
   (1887-1948)

GEORGE ARTHUR
(1852- ?)

WILLIAM THOMAS
(1857-1944)
Married
Isabella Jane McLellan
(1857-1951)

1. Edna Elizabeth
   Married
   Fred Wray Lambert
2. William Wilton
   (1888-1888)
3. George Grenville
   (1890-1970)
   Married
   Gertrude Scholey
4. Beatrice Belle
   (1893-1970)
   Married
   John Frank Lambert
   (1893-1963)
5. Leland Lawrence
   (1895-1958)
6. Caroline Clarice
   (1897-1969)

IV

FROM YEOMEN TO MANUFACTURERS

In common with other pioneer settlements, life in the Don Valley was constrained by the poor system of roads. It was easier for the farmers to travel in winter by horse and sleigh than to have to cope with the dust and mud at other times of the year. However, good access to the city was important and the residents of the valley decided to remedy the situation on their own. In December 1841,

> the inhabitants turned out with men and teams and commenced the construction of a road . . . and continued at it from day to day as voluntary labour until a passable road was made down to the Don and up the hill on the west side bounding what is now the Necropolis." [1]

That winter, timber was cut and, after a bridge was built in the spring, the road was opened to where it linked with Sumach Street. Helliwell's comment that when he was building a culvert he saw no one except the men he was working with and that the Hospital or Park reserve was covered in forest indicated how rural the area remained. [2]

The new road, which was built through land owned by John Scadding, the father of Dr. Henry Scadding, was connected to the Don Mills Road farther north and to the south it ran through a gully along the banks of the Don River. The residents soon objected that they were obliged to pay the same amount of money at the toll gate at the Don Bridge where their road met the Kingston Road as those who had travelled a much greater distance. In 1844, the year that William Helliwell was appointed Pathmaster of the Don Mills Road, their road needed to be improved. To pay for planking, a number of the inhabitants went into partnership and formed the Don Mills Road Company with a toll gate of their own. They signed a document entitled *The Articles of Partnership of the Don Mills Road Company,* and in it the Parties of the First Part were the Reverend Henry Scadding and Colley Foster, Esq., trustees of the estate of Mr. John Scadding; and the Parties of the Second Part were John Eastwood, William Helliwell and John Taylor. In the list of partners which followed, John and George Taylor were listed as yeomen and their brother Thomas as a butcher:

John Eastwood, Esq. Thomas Taylor, butcher
William Helliwell, brewer George Taylor, yeoman
John Taylor, yeoman Samuel Jacobs, yeoman
Joseph Helliwell, brewer William Dallimore, yeoman
Philip De Grassie, Esq. James Sampson, blacksmith
Richard C. Playter, yeoman John Lea, yeoman
William Lea, yeoman

William Dallimore, the Taylors' brother-in-law, was living in the valley at the time and only Phillipe De Grassie and John Eastwood were described as "Esquire" or gentleman.[3] The Don Mills Road Company was so successful that it constructed many streets still in use in the part of east Toronto known as Cabbagetown. Helliwell wrote years later:

We afterwards planked a street from the top of the hill to Parliament Street, which we named Bowen Street in honour of the man who gave the land. This corporation thought it proper to change it to Winchester Street. Immediately after this the cemetery was opened [i.e. St. James'] and Parliament Street planked by the corporation in 1842. The road from the forks of the Don to Milnes Mill was opened and made a public road for the benefit of the Upper Don settlement.[4]

He also remembered an amusing incident that is worth repeating in his own words:

When the Don Mills Road Company were grading and forming Parliament Street to receive the coating of plank with which it was covered, it had been necessary at one place to make a cutting of three or four feet deep, and one day a teamster of the Messrs. Taylor, a coloured man was driving a load of wood along the road and observed something shining in the fall of the cutting but being too indolent to dismount from his load of wood deferred to his return to make an examination. When doing so he found that a cow on climbing up the cutting had scraped the crystal off a gold watch and behind it was Mrs. Smith's jewellry which had lain buried for so many years.

Mrs. Smith's husband, William, had a tannery near the Don Bridge.

Mr. & Mrs. Smith were both dead but their son John laid claim to the property and proved it by the number of the watch being recorded on the books of Charles Clikunbroomer who had repaired it and taken down the number. He [Mr. Smith] and his wife were both at times in the habit of going on a drunken spree. I have myself put a fifteen gallon barrel of beer up by his bedside so he could reach it without getting out of bed where he lay and drank for days and weeks at a time. His wife would go off to the taverns and spree and drink for days. On one of these drinking bouts she took a small trunk containing £700 in cash, several notes, a gold watch and chain, several articles of jewellery and valuables with her and visited several taverns and remained away from home for several days carrying the trunk with her from place to place, and finally on arriving home and opening the trunk found only a few small bric brac. She had a tavern keeper by the name of Sherbourne taken up and put on his trial for robbery but there was no proof to convict him and he was discharged. [5]

It was during these years that the three Taylor brothers married, but as with their four sisters, we do not know the dates. John Taylor, the oldest, was married twice. His first wife, Anne Eliza Mundell, died giving birth to twin daughters (they also died) when she was thirty-two and he was left with two other daughters, Mary and Elizabeth Anne. [6] The latter died when she was nine and only Mary survived from this marriage. His second

John Taylor, the eldest son, 1809-1871.
Collection of George Taylor Gale

wife was Nancy Bright, a spinster of thirty-five who was one of the many daughters of Thomas and Jane Bright. It was a likely match since his brother George was already married to her sister Caroline and his friend William Helliwell had married two of

Nancy Bright Taylor, 1816-1896.
Collection of George Taylor Gale

her sisters. Nancy and John Taylor had two sons, John Hawthorne and Thomas Bright, and one daughter, Henrietta Jane. They lived in "Thorn Cliff", the house at the mill at the Forks of the Don which was the original Taylor home. [7]

Thorn Cliff, the Taylor's house at the Forks of the Don photographed by Audrey Taylor before 1940.
Collection of John Taylor

Thorn Cliff, photographed before it was demolished in the 1940s.
Todmorden Mills Archives

Thomas Taylor, 1811-1880.
Collection of Ross Wallace

    The second brother, Thomas, married Henrietta Jobbitt, a girl of seventeen, when he was thirty-five. [8] When there was such a discrepancy in the age of the bride and groom, it was often the occasion in pioneer days to hold a "charivari", a

Henrietta Jobbitt Taylor, 1829-1890.
Collection of Ross Wallace

Canadian custom which Susanna Moodie described in her book *Roughing It in the Bush*. The charivari took place on the wedding night when the young men of the community disguised themselves in masks or black-face and wearing "grotesque caps" decorated with cock's feathers and bells and went to the newlyweds' house. They made so much commotion, demanding to be let in to drink the health of the bride, that the groom was obliged to give them money to go and buy their toast at the local tavern. Few grooms dared to ignore the custom for it was well-known that such high spirits could get out of hand. More than one hapless groom had been tarred and feathered and ridden out of town on a rail. [9]

It is not surprising that Thomas and Henrietta had the largest family of their generation, thirteen children in all, and that when he died in 1881, at the age of sixty-nine, five were under the age of twenty-one with the youngest only seven. However, there was only one grandson to carry on this branch of the family. He was named William Thomas, the same name as the youngest son of his uncle George Taylor, but since he lived in the village of Homer, now part of St. Catherines, there never seems to have been any confusion between the two. This propensity for a common name occurred again when both Thomas and John Taylor named their second sons Thomas. To distinguish between the two, the family referred to Thomas' son as "Black Tom" and John's son as "White Tom" because of the colour of their hair.

The directories of the day listed only addresses for the city of Toronto and not for Todmorden where the Taylor brothers lived. Thomas was merely described as living on the Don Mills Road. After his death, his son, "Black Tom", built a large Victorian house for his mother and brothers and sisters on the site of the present 1132 Broadview Avenue. That house was called "Chester Park" when it was sold in 1888 to Robert Davies [10] and his family later sold it to the Salvation Army. They later demolished it and built a modern building on the site, but the original coach house at the back remains as a residence.

"Beechwood", the house where the youngest brother George and his wife Caroline lived, was built in 1840 [11] and is the oldest private house still standing in East York. Their first house was a frame dwelling which they replaced with the present Regency structure at 20 Beechwood Crescent. The front porch of the house has been demolished and the gracious lawns to the south have been subdivided into lots and houses, but the basic structure of the house is still visible.

Caroline Bright was first mentioned in William Helliwell's diaries when he took her for a walk when she was fifteen on April 15,1838—a cold day when they "went up the hill and wandered to Sinkleirs and returned by the short road above the mill dam". She probably married George at St. James' Cathedral, the Bright family church. They had a large family of three sons and five daughters. In 1863, when George was fifty, he commissioned Charles Loeffler, an American artist who lived in Toronto from 1857 to 1871, to paint their portraits along with his wife's mother, Jane Hunter Bright. [13]The portraits also indicated the improved status of the Taylors from yeomen in 1844 [14]to a family of means twenty years later. The same artist may have painted the handsome portrait of John Taylor Jr. which is in the

George Taylor, 1813-1894. Portrait painted by Charles Loeffler, 1863.
Author's collection

possession of his descendants, but only a photograph survives of the third brother, Thomas.

After Caroline Taylor died in 1868 at the age of forty-five, George decided to visit his birthplace in Staffordshire. He was the only one of the family to return to England. He took his oldest daughter Louise with him and while there he hoped to trace the origin of his mother-in-law's income of gold pieces. He was unsuccessful, however, and to the regret of the family never

Caroline Bright Taylor, 1823-1868. Portrait painted by Charles Loeffler, 1863.
Author's collection

discovered the source of her money. The family was left to conclude that on her death the money had been forfeited to the Crown, believing that such was the result ordained for unclaimed funds by the English Court of Chancery. George was successful, however, in finding a thirty-five-year-old bride named Annie Hollins. His children never liked her and blamed their sister for allowing the marriage to take place. Since she was only fifteen at the time, the accusation hardly seems fair. In the 1871 Census,

George Taylor and his family on the lawn of Beechwood in the 1880s showing their first frame house.
Collection of Mrs. E.G. LeGrice

Beechwood today, without the verandah. The oldest house in East York.
Todmorden Mills Archives

St. John's York Mills Anglican Church, 1817-1844, Old Yonge St., west side near Don Ridge Drive.
Metropolitan Toronto Public Library

the entire family of eight children, ranging from thirteen to twenty-four years of age, their step-mother, who was twenty years her husband's junior, and three servants were living at "Beechwood". Annie Hollins was never well-received, but perhaps her scrapbook of religious cuttings gave her some solace.

Some idea of the activities of the Taylors in the middle of the century may be obtained from an examination of the records of one of the parcels of land, Lot 15, Concession IIFB, which they purchased. It had been owned originally by that old-time resident of the valley, Samuel Sinclair. He first sold part of the land to the Taylors in 1839 [15] and the rest of the two-hundred acres to them in 1847 [16] except for ten acres. Sinclair gave one quarter of an acre to the Primitive Methodist Connexion for a church in 1851, but this deed cannot have been too clear because it was deeded to the church again in 1860 by the Taylors. They were Anglicans, not Methodists, and were associated with three churches, St. John's, York Mills; Little Trinity and the present Don Mills

Trinity Anglican Church, King St. E., south-west corner of Trinity St.
Metropolitan Toronto Public Library

United Church which was originally the Primitive Methodist Connexion.

Their names appear in the records of St. John's, York Mills, which they first attended when they lived in Vaughan Township, and some of them continued to have their children baptized there long after the family had moved to the Don Valley. In the history of the church written by Audrey Graham [17] there is a copy of a letter written in 1847 and signed by several members of the congregation, including John Taylor Jr. and W. and G. Lea, residents of the Don Valley, who expressed their appreciation to the minister, the Reverend Arthur Sanson, for conducting services at three distant out-stations. One was the south-east station which was held at the home of Henry G. Papst in the area of Eglinton and Bayview Avenues; and the third was held in the home of John Taylor at the Forks of the Don. For some time, these men had provided the minister with oats for his horse and as an expression of their appreciation for his services they informed him of their gift of a light wagon. [18] The Taylors thought so well of Mr. Sanson that when he moved to Little Trinity Anglican Church at King and Parliament Streets after its first minister, the Reverend W. H. Ripley, died of cholera, they joined that church.

The Don Mills United Church (demolished), built by the Taylor family for the Primitive Methodist Connexion.
Author's collection

Two of their brothers-in-law, William Gooderham and James Worts, who had married two Bright sisters, Margaret and Sarah, had helped found Little Trinity in 1842. Originally known as the "Poor Man's Church", it was built for the Protestant Irish who were not welcome at the Cathedral. Behind it Enoch Turner built the first free school for the poor in 1848. [19] Mr. Sanson served as rector of the church after 1852 and when George Taylor died in 1894, Sanson was one of the ministers at his funeral. [20] Much of Little Trinity was destroyed by fire in 1961, but funds were raised to restore it to its early proportions and it has been designated an historic site by the Ontario Government.

In time, there were so many Taylors that they attended several churches. When Edith and Margaret were married, they chose the Cathedral; some continued to attend Little Trinity and others became Methodists. This occurred because in the mid-century many of the Taylor employees were Methodists and

George Taylor himself was said to have thought that the Anglicans were becoming too high church. Thomas's wife, Henrietta, collected money for them [21] and many of the next generation joined the United Church of Canada at the time of church union in 1925.

The particular branch of Methodism that the family chose was the Primitive Methodist Connexion. This small off-shoot of British Wesleyans first met in York in 1829 in a school house on Duke Street. When their first preacher, William Watkins, came from England, he wrote that he found only "a small society of sixteen who had belonged to us and the Wesleyans in England". [22] They persevered and Watkin's successor, William Summersides, administered to a wide area including Scarborough and some places that are now forgotten— Woodhills, Blue Bells, Smith's, Centre Road, Churchville, Streetsville, Switzer's, Four Corners, Claridges, Paisley, Don Mills, Thornhill, Humber Halton and Hogg's Mills. He was assisted on the circuit by twelve local preachers and four exhorters, and the devotion he revealed in his diary of February 1832 was admirable: "the last thirteen days I have preached sixteen times...ridden fifty miles, walked seventy". [23]

When the three brothers and their wives gave land to the Primitive Methodist Connexion in 1860, [24] they also donated a brick church which became known as the Taylor Family Church. The first little frame building which had been used by the circuit preachers was moved to the east of the new building. The Taylor church was finally torn down in 1950 and replaced by the present Don Mills United Church at 126 O'Connor Drive at the corner of Pape Avenue.

Photographs and written accounts reveal the charm of the earlier brick church. Entry was through one of two front doors, the vestibule was lit by a window between the doors and was divided from the nave of the church by swinging doors covered in red baize. The church seated about one hundred people and there were two side aisles. Some of the pews had backs that could be turned over so that two rows could face each other and be used for the Sunday school. The Taylors occupied seats placed at right angles to the rest of the congregation at the front of the church in the manorial tradition and these were covered in red cushions. The altar table was also covered in red. The carpeting was red and the minister sat on a comfortable settee upholstered in red baize. Oil lamps were placed in single brackets between the side windows, in the three chandeliers hanging down the centre of the ceiling, and in the one over the organ, giving a charming effect to the interior. The choir and organ, which were originally inside the entrance on a raised platform behind the congregation, were later moved to the front of the church. The building was heated in winter by stoves.

Outside, the church property was surrounded by a white picket fence and, at the east, set well back from the road, was a driving shed to shelter the buggies and sleighs. There were two cemeteries, one for members of the church and the other, to the west, for the Taylors, [25] who still use it. It is now maintained by the Township of East York rather than by the family but title remains with the Taylor descendants.

In 1856, four years before they donated the church, John, Thomas and George and their wives sold part of an acre of Lot 15, Concession II FB to the trustees of school section number seven of the County of York for a "common school". [26] That was one way of ensuring that their children would attend school nearby. A one-room school with a belfry was erected on what is now the north-east corner of O'Connor Drive and Pape Avenue and it served the large area from Eglinton Avenue on the north to Danforth Avenue on the south, and from the Don Valley on the west to the boundary between York and Scarborough townships on the east. The school trustees were George Taylor, one of his Morse nephews and William Berry. "At one time twenty-three pupils attended classes under the direction of a teacher who was paid the princely sum of $12.00 per month and the parents paid 7 pence halfpenny per month, per child". [27] In 1879, another room was added to the school and the principal was paid $40.00 per month. Two years later the school was sold to David Smith, who married George Taylor's daughter Annie. They lived on property immediately north of the school in a house called "Pine Grove", which is now 1311 Pape Avenue. The school was later converted into a house where a family of market gardeners by the name of Mountain lived. [28]

The youngest sons of John and Thomas, Thomas Bright and Edmund were sent to Upper Canada College on King Street opposite Government House, while George's sons attended the

Annie Taylor Smith.
Collection of George Taylor Gale

Model School at the corner of Gould and Victoria Streets. The premises, which also housed the Ontario School of Art and the Normal School where teachers were trained, were described as "an ornament to the city" where, in addition to education, citizens could walk and enjoy the spacious grounds. [29] George's youngest son William liked to tell the story that when he was a student a group of his friends decided to play a trick on one of the boys whom they disliked. One by one they went up to him and asked him how he was feeling until he soon began to feel quite ill and had to go home. None of the Taylors of this generation received any further formal education—John and George's sons went into the family business; "Black Tom", Thomas's son, became a brewer and owned a farm near St. Catharines with his brother William Lewis, where they kept horses and had a race track; Edmund, the youngest, was also interested in horses and had his own business.

The real turning-point in the affairs of the Taylors occurred when they established a company called John Taylor and Brothers, Paper Manufacturers. The exact year that this came about is difficult to ascertain, but it seems generally accepted that the company was started in 1845 and that the following year a paper mill was built on the west branch of the river at the Forks of the Don near their saw and grist mills. [30] The impetus for this was provided by George Brown who was in need of a local supply of newsprint for *The Globe,* and who arranged to have a paper-making machine shipped from Edinburgh and installed at the new mill. [31]

Brown and his father Peter had come to Toronto in 1843 at the invitation of the Free Kirk to set up a weekly newspaper, *The Banner,* to express the views of Free Church Presbyterianism. Peter Brown had been reluctant to leave New York, where he published the *British Chronicle,* but gave way to his son's enthusiasm for Toronto, which he described as "the chief commercial centre and the largest city in Canada West". [32] At that time, the population of the city was 16,000, but as young Brown wrote to his father:

The country is young, there are few persons of ability and education. There is no position a man of energy and character may not reasonably hope to attain if his will be strong and his brain sound. [33]

Once *The Banner* was in circulation, George Brown was approached by "a group of prominent Reformers to found a new political journal" and before he was twenty-six, he was the editor and publisher of *The Globe.* It shared the same premises as *The Banner* at 142 King Street. *The Globe* was in direct competition with five other political journals: *The Examiner, The Mirror, The Herald, The Patriot* and *The British Colonist,* but it managed to be very successful. Within two years, it was on the streets three times a week and a regional edition entitled *The Western Globe* or *The London, Western and Huron District Advertiser* was being distributed in Southwestern Ontario.

An immediate supply of newsprint was crucial and this was provided by the Taylor mill in the Don Valley. The process of making paper was a tedious operation requiring at least ten men and boys to run the various types of machinery. Paper was made from a raw stock of rags and, from the earliest days of paper-making in Upper Canada, this presented a serious problem. In 1826, William Lyon Mackenzie had advertised in the *Colonial*

Advocate that cash would be paid for rags [35] which, it should be pointed out, were not of linen, which made the best paper, but of homespun wool and cotton.

Straw and jute were added to the rags and later esparto grass was substituted, but none were satisfactory and the paper was of poor quality. The raw stock had to be sorted after it was accumulated and then it was cooked in a liquor made of soda and lime that was boiled and left to settle. The straw was drawn off and cooked in another vat. This is the process that George Brown is said to have taught the Taylors. [36]

John, the oldest of the three brothers, was the manager of the mill and was reported to have had a talent for mechanics and a flair for invention. [37] In 1854, a reward of £1,000 was offered in London, England, to anyone who could find a substitute for rags as a raw source for paper. Whether or not this was the reason, John Taylor was reported to have applied for a patent for making paper out of wood pulp and it is believed that some paper was actually made at the mill using basswood. To do this he:

> mounted knives on a wheel to shave off the wood and then he used a gang of saws mounted on a mandrel about ten feet long which moved to and fro at right angles to the grain of the wood. His next plan was a chisel-like machine very much like a chipper except when it moved up and down. [38]

These innovations have earned him the little-known honour of being one of the originators of the technical development of the paper industry in Canada. [39]

The three brothers were a good combination. John managed the mill; Thomas looked after the business office that they opened at 30 Market Square; [40] and George was in charge of their farming and lumbering operations. In time, they owned three mills in the Don Valley which were called the Upper, Middle and Lower Mills. Much of the information regarding the acquisition of the Middle and Lower Mills is contradictory. The Census of 1851 indicated that a second mill was in the process of being built. This must have been the Middle Mill on Lot 10, Concession II. [41] However, the generally accepted view is that they purchased the Lower Mill in 1855, which was so named

The Taylor Paper Mills.
Toronto Illustrated, Past and Present

Map showing the Taylor property.
Historical Atlas of York County, Miles and Company, 1878

because of its location two miles south on the river, and that they built the Middle Mill in 1858.[42] The Lower, or York Paper Mill, as it was first called, was of particular historical interest to Upper Canada. Originally the old Skinner grist mill, it had been converted into a paper mill by John Eastwood, Colin Skinner and an experienced paper maker called Robert Stonehouse.

Just as George Brown had encouraged the Taylors, so had William Lyon Mackenzie provided the impetus for this mill in 1825. At this time, newsprint was imported from the United States and the United Kingdom. It was quite apparent to Mackenzie that a local paper industry was sorely needed to reduce the costs entailed by high tariffs and limited supply. He wrote: "If the government offered liberal encouragement to a paper maker he would have saved us £3,000 Halifax a year...".[43]

A petition, which he initiated at a meeting at the Masonic Lodge in York, asking for assistance to establish a local industry, was presented to the Legislature. Its members readily acquiesced and agreed to offer £125 to the first person to successfully manufacture paper. [44] This incentive encouraged James Crooks of Crook's Hollow in West Flamborough, near Hamilton, to add a paper mill to his already growing complex of mills and shops and he won the bounty. [45] In close competition was the York Paper Mill under the management of John Eastwood, Skinner and Stonehouse. These three men placed an advertisement in *The Colonial Advocate:*

YORK PAPER MILL

The subscribers, having entered into co-partnership, for the purposes of converting the Don Mill into a paper mill, and having most of the mill-wright done, and also a considerable stock of rags collected, they will lose no time in completing and carrying it into operation. One of the partners, having had many years experience in the business, both in England and the United States, they flatter themselves that they will be able to make a good article, which they intend to sell as cheap as it can be had from the State of New York. They earnestly solicit the patronage of the public and hope all persons will feel an interest in saving the RAGS, as they have persons appointed to collect the same, who will call regularly and give the highest price for them.

    John Eastwood Colin Skinner
      Robert Stonehouse

[46]

They were also successful and by the fall of 1828 both the Crooks Mills and the York Paper Mill were making paper. Although the Crooks Mill won the bounty, the government gave Eastwood and Skinner another concession in recognition of their efforts. They had imported the first paper-making machine from the United States and when they protested, the government agreed to remit the import duty as their reward. [47]

Mackenzie used Eastwood and Skinner's paper for his *Colonial Advocate,* but thought it was of such inferior quality that he was obliged to write:

> We have to apologize for the bad quality of paper furnished by Messrs. Eastwood and Skinner. Our reader may rely upon it that as soon as we can remedy the evil we will not fail to do so . . . [48]

The "evil" evident in the edition of January 4, 1834 was probably "fishtail" and striation marks the experts now think may have been caused by the paper manufacturer's newly installed press and driers. [49]

Eastwood left the partnership and went into politics, representing St. Lawrence Ward in 1836; he later was a magistrate and, in partnership with W.G. Edmundson, purchased *The Canadian Farmer and Mechanic,* which they published in Toronto. Elizabeth Taylor's son, William Mills Morse, married Eastwood's daughter Elizabeth on Christmas Day in 1854. Colin Skinner managed the mill until his death in 1841, and his cousin Joseph purchased it. In 1855, he sold it to the Taylors. [50]

John Taylor and Brothers, Paper Manufacturers were riding a wave of expansion in the paper industry in the 1850s. Not only had the population of Toronto risen to well over thirty thousand, but it was also more literate. Like ripples on a pond, as education became more common the larger reading public demanded more books and newspapers. At the same time, the new telegraph system broadened the reporting of the news and the expanding railway network gave a much wider distribution to newspapers. Over all, the Province had 172 newspapers and the publishing business had clearly become more complex. [51] The Taylor mills kept pace with these developments and by the 1870s they were operating around the clock with an enormous capacity.

A description of the firm listed in *Toronto, Past and Present* stated that they supplied "a very large proportion of the printing paper now used for the daily and weekly papers of this city and throughout the Dominion" from Newfoundland to the Red River. In addition, they also manufactured other varieties of paper, including "coloured paper for poster bills, also all kinds of books, manillas, roll, expressing, tea and common papers and paper bags". [52]

The Middle Mill is still in operation today as part of the Don Valley Division of Domtar, but unfortunately all of the early records were destroyed during hurricane Hazel in 1954. The Census records show that in 1851 the Taylors employed 15 people at the Upper Mill and in the 1871 Census, when the three mills were in operation, there were 62 employees. It is difficult to assess the worth of their operations by today's values; the best one can do is to relate the aggregate annual wages of the company, which were $8,000 for sixty-two people, to the capital investment of $80,000 and a floating capital of $10,000.

John Taylor reported that the three mills were worked as one integrated factory and George Carruthers in *Paper in the Making* confirmed this analysis of the Taylor operations. A former employee, W.J. Russell, told Carruthers that he was employed by the Taylors as a "lay" boy when he was ten years old and that his father had been the foreman at the Upper Mill. It is interesting that the Taylor firm employed six boys and three girls under the age of sixteen and of those employees over that age, eight were women and forty-five were men.

John Taylor died unexpectedly on May 13, 1871 at the age of sixty-two from "an acute inflamation". [53] As was expected in those days, he had endured his suffering with "Christian resignation and fortitude". The laudatory obituary in *The Globe* claimed that it was largely through his efforts that "the great extension of the family firm was due". [54] Before he died, the Census-takers in 1871 had asked him for details of the family enterprises. In addition to the paper mills, he reported that the family had a large mixed farming operation and that 300 cattle had been slaughtered that year. The family always maintained that they were the first to ship beef cattle to England from Upper Canada. The year of the census, their dairy operation also produced 800 pounds of butter and 300 pounds of cheese and from their sheep they received 120 pounds of wool. They also raised pigs on their farms. Most revealing, the family land holdings consisted of 3,811 acres, 10 building lots, 35 houses, 3 warehouses and 27 barns and stables—a most impressive increase in less than forty years from their father's original purchase of 82 acres in the Don Valley. Their land transactions were so extensive and convoluted that it would be nearly impossible to search them all in the Registry Office, but the general assumption has been that they owned land up the valley from the Forks of the Don to Eglinton Avenue and the corner of the present Don Mills Road and south as far as Todmorden. It was gratifying that John Taylor Sr., the original settler, was able to witness the achievements of his sons before he died at about ninety years of age. This vigorous old man was buried in the family cemetery and has a handsome stone monument to his memory.

During the years that the Taylor brothers were consolidating their land holdings and expanding the mills in the Don Valley, many changes were taking place. They had set up an office and a warehouse near the St. Lawrence Market in Toronto, and were described as paper manufacturers and flour dealers in the *Toronto Directory*. This was a far cry from twenty years earlier, when John and George were classed as yeomen and Thomas as a butcher.

Notes

1. (TMA), Memorandums of William Helliwell, (n.p., 1896) p. 11.
2. *Ibid.,* p. 12.
3. (TMA), file x973.103, A-6, 15 May, 1844.
4. (TMA), Memorandums of William Helliwell, (n.p., 1896) p. 12.
5. *Ibid.,* pp. 18-19.
6. Taylor Family Cemetery, Don Mills United Church, Toronto.
7. *Toronto Directory,* 1859-60, p. 188.
8. Ross Wallace, "Eight Score Years and Twelve" (Orillia, unpublished, 1973), genealogy of the Thomas Taylor family.
9. Susanna Moodie, *Roughing It in the Bush* (Toronto: McClelland and Stewart, 1923), p. 229.
10. R.O. #26360, 28 January, 1888.
11. (TMA), Inventory of Historical Buildings in East York, p. 17.
12. In the possession of the author, drawing on an invitation in 1885.
13. Russell Harper, *Early Painters and Engravers in Canada* (Ottawa: National Gallery of Canada, 1963), p. 200.

14. (TMA), Articles of Partnership of the Don Mills Road Company, file x973.103, A-6, 15 May 1844.
15. R.O. #16543, Old York Books, 1839.
16. R.O. #30398, 1847.
17. M.A. Graham, *150 Years at St. John's, York Mills* (Toronto: General Publishing Co., Ltd., 1966), p. 124.
18. *Ibid.,* p. 124.
19. Little Trinity Church, pamphlet, "Welcome to Little Trinity".
20. Obituary, Family Scrapbook, source unknown.
21. Wallace, p. 9.
22. Don Mills United Church, pamphlet, "United Summer Services, July and August, 1966".
23. *Ibid.*
24. R.O. #80864, 1860.
25. Edna Ash, "The Don Mills United Church", n.p., n.d.
26. R.O. #64056, 1856.
27. Ash, "Early Chester and Todmorden Schools" (n.p., n.d.)
28. *Ibid.*
29. E.P. Mulvany, *Toronto Past and Present* (Toronto: W.E. Caiger, 1884; Toronto Reprint Press, 1970), p. 86.
30. *Dictionary of Canadian Biography* (Toronto: University of Toronto Press), v. X, 1982, p. 671.
31. (TMA), Charles Sauriol, "The Story of the Don" (n.p., n.d.) File x973.344, p. 41.
32. J.M.S. Careless, *Brown of the Globe* (Toronto: MacMillan & Co., Ltd., 1959), 2 vols, v. I, p. 24.
33. *Ibid.,* p. 22.
34. *Ibid.,* p. 41.
35. J.A. Blyth, "The Development of the Paper Industry in Old Ontario, 1824 - 1867", *Ontario History,* LXII, June, 1970, p. 121.
36. George Carruthers, *Paper in the Making* (New Jersey: Garden City Press, 1947), p. 310.
37. Ibid., p. 311.
38. *Ibid.,* p. 311.
39. Blyth, p. 133.

40. J. Temperlake, *Illustrated Toronto, Past and Present* (Toronto: Peter A. Gross, 1977), p. 283.
41. Ian Howes, "A History of Paper Making in the Don Valley" (unpublished research paper), p. 19.
42. Carruthers, p. 308.
43. Blyth, p. 119.
44. *Ibid.*, p. 120.
45. *Ibid.*, p. 120.
46. Carruthers, p. 298, quoting the *Colonial Advocate*, April 17, 1826.
47. Carruthers, p. 307.
48. *Ibid.*, p. 308.
49. *Ibid.*, p. 300.
50. *Ibid.*, p. 305.
51. Blyth, p. 127.
52. Temperlake, p. 282.
53. *The Globe* (Toronto), May 15, 1871.
54. *Ibid.*

V

Prosperity

By 1851, the Don Valley had passed from pioneer isolation into a mature rural community closely tied to Toronto's development. Toronto had also changed into an important commercial centre with a population of 30,775. Its Victorian sophistication was sufficient to welcome the Prince of Wales when he arrived on September 7, 1860 on the battleship "Hero". That event heralded the vigour of the decade with colourful pageantry. A crowd of ten thousand turned out to greet His Royal Highness at the Mayor's reception and for an entire week, he was enthusiastically received as he visited public buildings, planted trees, attended a ball in his honour at the Crystal Palace (located due south of 999 Queen Street West), and a church service at St. James' Cathedral where Bishop Strachan preached.

The decade between 1850 and 1860 was the beginning of the great expansion of railways. New areas were opened, land prices soared, manufacturing expanded, employment was high and for six years trade and commerce flourished. However, in 1857 the railway boom collapsed. Huge debts had been incurred from over-expansion and land speculation and the commercial crisis in Britain and the United States spread to Canada causing a severe depression. Naturally, it affected the banks. In 1850, new legislation endeavoured to make some improvements in the field of banking. The Free Bank Act provided for "free banks" with easier access to credit and was an attempt to reduce the power of the few large chartered banks, chief of which were the Bank of Montreal, the Commercial Bank and the Bank of Upper Canada. The new policy of handing out charters with little regard for the credentials of the applicants encouraged promoters interested only in a quick profit. There were bankruptcies and some shocking abuses of the financial system. The

First Head Office of the Bank of Commerce (1867-1890), south-east corner of Yonge and Colbourne Streets, formerly occupied by the Bank of Upper Canada.
Ontario Archives

government soon recognized that the system of large chartered banks with branch offices was preferable to small local banks with limited capital. The Bank of Toronto received its charter in 1855 and by 1857, twelve other banks had been incorporated.

The Bank of Upper Canada, regarded as the bulwark of the financial system in old Ontario since its establishment in 1825 was badly affected by the depression of 1857. It had invested heavily in land, railways and milling enterprises and when the provincial government transferred its account to its rival, the Bank of Montreal, the public lost confidence in it and it failed in 1866. Similarly, the Kingston-based Commercial Bank was forced to close its doors. This left the Bank of Montreal paramount in the field of banking, but it was not well-regarded in Canada West. In particular, it was criticized for giving preference to Montreal and New York interests.

Mechanics' Institute, Church Street, north-east corner of Adelaide Street East.
Metropolitan Toronto Public Library

Something had to be done and some of the members of the Toronto business community decided to establish a new bank. Not all of the charters that had been granted had been taken up and "some lay in abeyance through their inability to raise the necessary capital". [1] One of these was the Bank of Canada. William McMaster, after whom the university in Hamilton is named, purchased its charter and changed its name to The Canadian Bank of Commerce when the Governor General, Viscount Monck, gave his assent on August 15, 1866.

It was not until the following February, however, that "the necessary committees were formed and the work of organization was taken up actively". [2] When the new directors were chosen at the first meeting of the shareholders held in the Mechanics Institute at the corner of Church and Adelaide Streets, John Taylor was prominent enough in the business community to be elected to the board. "He had become a public figure in a minor way, as a leader of the Toronto Branch of the Reform Association of Upper Canada, reconstituted in 1867, and as a member of the coterie surrounding [George] Brown, became a founding director." [3]

McMaster was president, Henry S. Howland was vice-president, and the other directors in addition to John Taylor were William Alexander, T. Sutherland Stayner, William Elliot and John Macdonald. These men were described in the history of the Bank of Commerce as men who had "a solid stake in the community to whom improved banking conditions were vital". [4] John Taylor served as a director for four years until his death in 1871, at which time his brother George took his place. This trend of appointing relatives and close associates was continued over the years. For example, McMaster's nephew A. R. McMaster and Henry Darling, who were both associated with the McMaster wholesale business, came on the board. William Gooderham, another director, was a nephew of the Taylors and, much later, George Cox brought his good friend and business partner Sir Joseph Flavelle to the board.

From the beginning, the new bank was well-received by the public. Branches in London, St. Catharines and Barrie were authorized and requests for branches in other towns were considered. Before the first year was completed, the directors declared a dividend of 8½% and at the first annual meeting excellent progress was reported. The shareholders voted permission to apply to Parliament to increase the capital stock to two million dollars and the following year the bank amalgamated with the Gore Bank, the first of five the Commerce absorbed. A head-office building was purchased at the corner of Yonge and Colborne Streets, once occupied by the Bank of Upper Canada, and a corporate seal, designed and executed by the Toronto engraver Joseph T. Rolph, was chosen. When the Bank of Montreal opened an office in London, England, the board, not wishing to be outdone by its major rival, sent McMaster to make similar arrangements for the Bank of Commerce. He was not successful, however, and the bank had to be satisfied with the arrangements he made with the Bank of Scotland in Edinburgh. As chairman, McMaster's policies were not always well-received. John Macdonald, the so-called Merchant Prince of Toronto, left the board over a difference of opinion with him after only three months. James Austin, who took his place, was also dissatisfied with McMaster's direction and resigned at the annual meeting of 1870. He subsequently joined the Dominion Bank. McMaster was intent on expanding the bank's assets and within four years of its founding, he had received authorization to increase the bank's capital to six times its original amount. Toronto was now on its was to becoming a serious threat to Montreal's domination of the financial scene in Canada.

George Taylor, the second member of the family to serve on the bank's board, remained as a director for twenty-three years until his death in 1894. George was associated with a formidable group of Toronto businessmen. The Hon. William McMaster, perhaps best known as the founder of McMaster University, retired in 1886. He was a member of the first Senate of Canada, a position that was very helpful when banking legislation was under consideration in Parliament. A staunch Baptist and founder of Jarvis Street Baptist Church, it is understandable that he did not stay for a glittering reception at Rideau Hall in honour of the Duke of Connaught where over nine hundred bottles of wine were consumed by the two thousand guests. His letter to the Directors stated that after making "three of his best bows" he left. [5] At the time of his retirement, the bank had been going through a bad time; its assets had shrunk by almost 20% and its reserves had been depleted to meet the bad debts incurred when a number of its wealthy customers were ruined through the collapse of land prices in the Northwest.

McMaster proposed George A. Cox to the board. He too was a self-made man who had started as a telegraph operator in Peterborough and eventually became one of the most powerful men in Canada. Perhaps George Taylor and his wife were invited to attend some of the lavish parties at "Sherbourne Villa", the large white brick house with extensive grounds that Cox purchased in 1888. [6] Senator Cox was a financial wizard and at one time was either president, vice-president or a director of forty-six companies.

Another outstanding Canadian with whom George would have been familiar was Byron Edmund Walker, who was brought back from the New York branch of the bank to be general manager in 1866 when he was only thirty-eight. The shining star of the bank, he was not only an expert on banking and financial questions, but also is remembered as an art connoisseur and the founder of Canada's great art institutions, the National Gallery in Ottawa, the Art Gallery of Ontario and the Royal Ontario Museum. Charles Trick Currelly, who knew him well, said that he had an extraordinary power of creating enthusiasm. "His smile was a great asset to any institution in which he was interested. Few men have been more eager for the development of his country or more eager to learn all they could about works of art". [7] A truly outstanding man, he was also prominent in the affairs of the University of Toronto, the Canadian Institute, the Champlain Society and the Mendelssohn Choir. He was knighted in 1910.

During those Victorian years when the bank was getting started, bank clerks were required to take their turn on guard duty and were paid fifty cents a night. One of them was so frightened when he was awakened in the middle of the night by a policeman standing over him shining a lantern in his face because he had left the door of the bank unlocked, that he forgot to reach for the revolver under his pillow. Even after World War I, a grandson of George Taylor's who worked for the bank described being driven through the Don Valley with a night deposit beside him on the seat of the car and a revolver in his pocket in case they were held up. Another incident illustrates how much was expected of bankers in those days. On Monday, February 25, 1886, a messenger went into the vault of the Toronto office to investigate a report of leaking gas; not smelling any, he lit a match to light the gas burners and the resulting explosion broke all but one window, shook the joists and partitions, and damaged the heavy iron door of the vault. Some of the staff were cut by flying glass, but business was suspended for only two hours.

When George Taylor died, such was his long association with the Bank of Commerce that three of the directors, George A. Cox, Robert Kilgour and W. H. Beatty, were among the pallbearers at his funeral. His long life had spanned the pioneering of Upper Canada and the maturing of one of the great financial institutions of the country.

After John Taylor died in 1871, the name of the family paper-manufacturing firm was changed to Thomas Taylor and Brother [8] and the business carried on with continued success. John's will stated that his two sons, John Hawthorne and Thomas Bright,

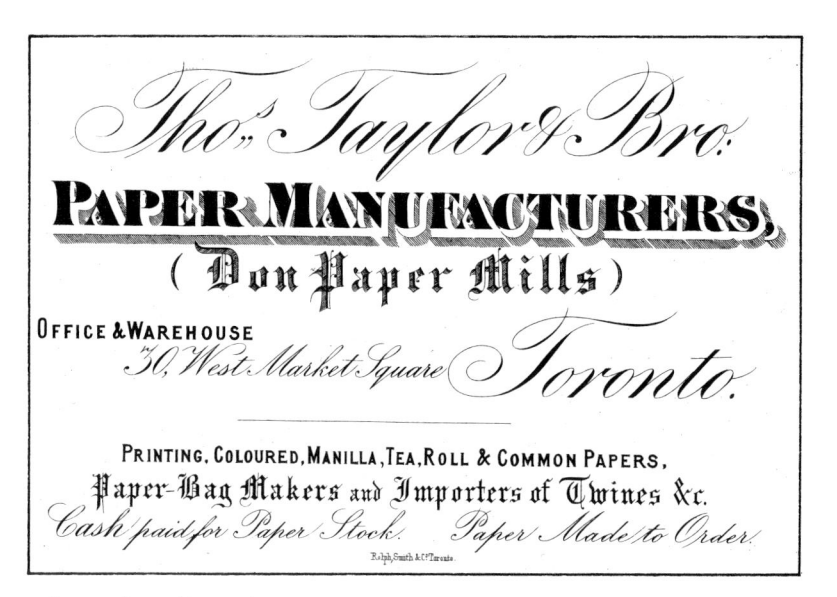

> **Thos Taylor & Bro.**
> **PAPER MANUFACTURERS**
> (Don Paper Mills)
> OFFICE & WAREHOUSE
> 30 West Market Square — Toronto.
>
> PRINTING, COLOURED, MANILLA, TEA, ROLL & COMMON PAPERS.
> Paper-Bag Makers and Importers of Twines &c.
> Cash paid for Paper Stock.   Paper Made to Order.
>
> Ralph, Smith & Co. Toronto

Collection of Ronald R. Tasker

who were fourteen and eight at the time of their father's death, were not to inherit their father's third interest in the partnership and his real estate until they had each reached the age of twenty-five.[9] This provision gave their uncles time to rearrange their affairs.

John H. (as he was known) went into the family business and worked as manager of the Upper Mill. Like his father, he was enterprising and rebuilt the mill with new machinery from Philadelphia in 1876. When he was interviewed by *The Star* many years later, he described supplying *The Globe* with newsprint in sheets, not rolls, and said that the output of the mill in his day averaged 1,500 pounds per day.[10] George Brown was also buying newsprint from the Riordan plant at Merriton near St. Catharines. John Riordan, a dynamic Irishman who is recognized as the father of the pulp and paper industry in Canada,[11] had established his factory in 1861. He had been the first to install a Fourdrinier machine, and by 1868 was able to produce ten tons of paper per day. This was formidable competition for the Taylors and John H. realized the need to move with the times. For instance, he recognized the tremendous advantages of harnessing the power at Sault Ste. Marie twenty years before it was actually developed, and suggested that the family should

John Hawthorne Taylor (1853-1940) and family.
Author's collection

relocate their mills, but his uncles and cousins who were then in the business would not consider it. The mills on the Don were doing well and were in full production.

They were supplying newsprint to customers across the Dominion and were manufacturing a diverse variety of paper products and importing twine. [12] However, they advertised that they "employed no travellers", [13] which may have been a mistake. An incident which John H. described to George Carruthers when he was preparing his book, *Paper in the Making*, was one of life's amusing coincidences:

> One evening when he [John H.] was attending the theatre a man sat next to him and seeing that he had made his programme into a paper maker's hat, he asked if he were not of the persuasion. During the conversation, the stranger told him that he too was a paper maker having a mill in the Highlands and invited him to make a short visit and do some shooting. Mr. Taylor accepted and was delightfully entertained and made the further discovery that his host was interested in buying Canadian lumber. When he asked

114

Thomas Bright Taylor, "White Tom", 1857-1903.
Collection of George Taylor Gale

Mr. Taylor if he knew anything about lumber, the latter replied that he owned a sawmill within a few hundred yards of his house and he invited his host to visit him in Canada. Shortly afterwards, the Scotsman arrived in Toronto and Mr. Taylor took him out to watch the lumbering operations. The logs were stamped with the owner's or buyer's mark, and to his surprise, Mr. Taylor found that his visitor was the owner of the mark he had been using and that, without knowing it, they had been doing business for some time. [14]

In 1878, the Taylor firm won an Honourable Mention for its paper at the Paris Exposition and the following year its paper received three gold medals at the Toronto Exposition. [15] In 1880, the firm was listed as both paper-bag manufacturers and paper manufacturers. There were about 100 girls making bags by hand. When John H. was urged to let them go and install bag-making machinery, he refused and lost a great business opportunity to Joseph Kilgour, who installed the machinery and took over the paper bag business. [16]

The year 1880 was another turning point in the family affairs. Thomas, who was the business manager, retired at the age of sixty-nine and his brother George, who was two years younger, decided that he too should step down. Management of the business fell to the next generation, composed of their brother John's two sons, John H. and T. B. or "White Tom", and George's three sons, John F., George A. and William Thomas. None of Thomas' three sons went into the business. "Black Tom" was twenty-seven and William Lewis was nineteen at the time of the new partnership, and could have been included, but Edmund was only seven and by the time he came of age the firm was no longer thriving. Within two weeks of his retirement, Thomas died unexpectedly of typhoid fever. [17]

It was at this time that the large Victorian house known as "Chester Park" on Broadview Avenue was built and it was here that Henrietta and her children lived until 1888 when the house was sold and they moved to Jarvis Street. Their first house on Jarvis Street (number 466) no longer exists, but their second house (number 510) may be seen complete with its Victorian porches and stained glass windows. Austin Thompson has described Jarvis Street of that era as "the Champs Elysees of Toronto resplendent with its side walks and ornamental fences and its great shade trees". [18] It was here that "the upper ten" resided, [19] but it is more likely that Henrietta and her family were only quiet observers of the socially prominent Masseys who lived across the street. It was in this house that she died after a long illness at the age of sixty-two in 1890. [20]

Her son Thomas, "Black Tom", who was the secretary-treasurer of the Ontario Brewing and Malting Company, went to live above the brewery and married one of the employees. This was not quite the thing to do, but, as the family said, there were

Thomas Taylor,
"Black Tom," 1853-1913.
Collection of Ross Wallace

Chester Park (demolished) 1132 Broadview Avenue. Henrietta Taylor built this house after the death of her husband Thomas.
Collection of Ross Wallace

John Frederick Taylor, 1849-1901.
Collection of George Taylor Gale

no children from the marriage. He and his brother William Lewis owned a farm together at Homer where they kept race horses and had their own race track. William Lewis died there when he was only thirty-five from a disease which was thought to have been contracted from one of the horses. His only son William Thomas was born posthumously. He became a farmer and his descendants still live in the area of St. Catharines. "Black Tom" later contracted cancer and retired to the farm where he died in 1913. Edmund, Henrietta's youngest son, became a partner in the Hodgson-Taylor Cartage Company and was its president when he died in 1944. [21]

The new family firm of Taylor Brothers wasted no time making changes and William Helliwell spoke of being taken by

George Arthur Taylor, b. 1852.
Collection of George Taylor Gale

William Thomas Taylor, 1857-1944.
Collection of George Taylor Gale

George Taylor to see "the great improvements in rebuilding the Mill and Houses". The firm consisted of John F., George Arthur and William Thomas (George's sons) and perhaps for a few years their cousins John H. and "White Tom". It is difficult to ascertain whether they were all in partnership together because John Taylor's two sons centred their activities around the Upper Mill. It is possible that they marketed the products of this mill with those from the other two and were part of the family firm. However, by 1889, John H. had left the mill and become a farmer and cattle breeder. In 1890, the Upper Mill closed.

Once the new generation of Taylors had their inheritance under their control, they took up a style of living commensurate with their position in society. They built large Victorian mansions and lived graciously. It was the time of large families, Irish servants, horses and sleighs, gigs, church-going and visiting cards. The area around Todmorden was still rural, of course, with dusty roads and only Don Mills Road as the main thoroughfare to the city. It ran parallel to the Don Valley to the west and south and passed through the now forgotten villages of Chester and Doncaster. One resident remembered it with nostalgia:

William Lewis Taylor, 1861-1896.
Collection of Ross Wallace

Edmund Taylor, 1873-1944.
Collection of Kathryn Dowthwaite

> In winter the road was smooth with snow packed down by sleigh runners, in spring ankle-deep in mud, in summer thick with fine dust. At intersections boards were laid for crossings. On each side of the road were deep ditches, their sides lush in summer with tall grasses, wild rose bushes, buttercups, daisies and meadowsweet. Along one side of the road ran a board walk. In places great trees—among them magnificent chestnuts—spread over in summer shade. Along both sides red brick or white frame houses, their front yards usually enclosed by picket fences, were scattered singly in groups or in rows, separated by fields of grass and clover or by vacant lots. Through the open spaces on the west side could be seen the quiet woods on the sides and crest of the Don Valley and the lovely sunsets beyond. [22]

Four Oaks Gate (demolished), corner of Don Mills Road and O'Connor Drive, John H. Taylor's house.
Collection of George Taylor Gale

John H. and his wife Matilda McLean had nine children and lived their long married life at "Four Oaks Gate", a large Victorian house of pleasing proportions set well back from the north-east corner of Don Mills Road and O'Connor Drive. Thomas Bright Taylor married Henrietta Victoria Davies in 1880. She was one of the daughters of Thomas Davies, who owned a brewery in the lower part of the valley near Queen Street. Their wedding took place from her family homestead on River Street at the unusual hour of six o'clock in the morning because they were leaving on the seven o'clock boat for Niagara for their honeymoon. [23] It was a good match since a few months earlier Thomas had inherited his share of his father's estate. [24] The inheritance was a six hundred acre parcel of land at the Forks of the Don (parts of Lots 6, 7, 8, and 9, Concession III FB) and a share of the Upper Mill. [25] Thomas used the estate as collateral to raise considerable amounts of cash. Like all the Taylors, his affairs were complicated, especially in the area of land transactions, but it is of passing interest that Henry Cawthra and Elias Rogers, two well-known Toronto businessmen, knew him well enough to give him mortgages. [26]

Matilda McLean Taylor
(Mrs. John H.).
Collection of George Taylor Gale

Edith, Audrey, Dorothy and Jessie, daughters of John H. Taylor.
Author's collection

Taylor Brothers' office, Market Square West, Toronto.
Author's collection

Don Mills Road, Todmorden, 12th of July Parade, 1911.
Todmorden Mills Archives

Henrietta Victoria Davies Taylor (Mrs. T.B.), 1857-1944.
Collection of George Taylor Gale

It was not long before the beautiful Henrietta Victoria decided that living in the country at "Thorn Cliff", the family house, was much too quiet and she persuaded her husband to build a house at 180 Sherbourne Street at the south-west corner of Shuter Street. About this time, Thomas became the vice-president of the Ontario Brewing and Malting Company owned by his brother-in-law William Thomas and continued to maintain his interest in the paper mill. In 1887, he went into partnership with William Selby. Both men were listed under Selby and Company as wholesale paper makers and stationers with kindergarten school supplies at 33-35 Scott Street. The following year, he sold all his valley property, including mortgages, [27] to his brother-in-law Robert Davies for $50,000 and in 1890 his connections with the Don Valley ended when the Upper Mill closed. After that, he was described as a traveller for the Dominion Brewery. [28] He and Henrietta lived at 33 River Street from 1891 until 1896, after which he rented Robert Davies'

William Gooderham House, 367 Sherbourne Street, north-east corner of Sherbourne and Carlton Streets.
Collection of George Taylor Gale

house at 397 Sherbourne Street. That house had originally belonged to William Gooderham. This latter move was to appease Henrietta's desire to live at the "society" end of the street. However, it led to family friction; Robert Davies was notorious for never missing an opportunity to make money even from members of his own family. Thomas, in order to placate his wife, was forced to pay Davies an exhorbitant rent. Thomas later bought the Copland Brewery at 55 Parliament Street and was president of it and the Ontario Brewing and Malting Company when he died at the age of forty-six in 1903. [29]

John F. Taylor, George's oldest son, was the business manager of Taylor Brothers until he retired because of ill health at the turn of the century. He died shortly after at the age of fifty-four. He was living at "Beechwood", his father's house, when the Census was taken in 1871 and did not marry until he was thirty-five. His bride was Lizzie Patterson, one of the daughters of Peter Patterson, a prominent manufacturer and local politician in Vaughan Township. He was also a member of the Ontario Legislature from 1871 to 1883. Like the Taylors of East York, the

Copland Brewery.
Toronto Illustrated, Past and Present

T.B. Taylor, President of the Copland Brewery.
Collection of George Taylor Gale

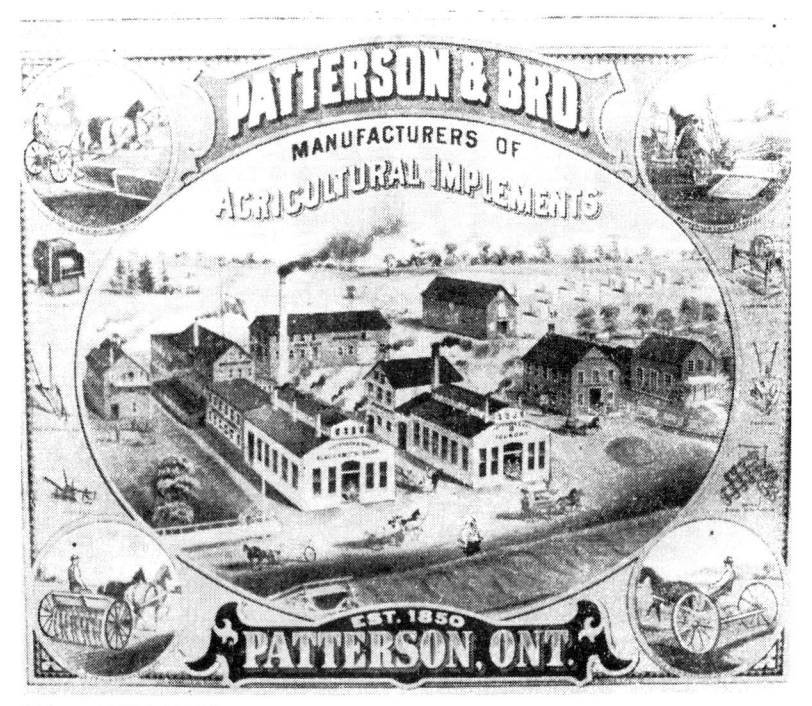

Richmond Hill Public Library

Pattersons were regarded as local gentry despite their humble beginnings.

Patterson and his two brothers, Alfred and Robert, came to Canada from New Hampshire sometime in the 1840s in order to sell Peter's invention of a fanning mill—a machine for screening grain. They moved from London to Dundas before they set up their firm of Patterson and Brother, Manufacturers of Agricultural Implements, in Richmond Hill at the corner of Richmond and Yonge Streets. They were so successful that they were able to buy 100 acres on the Vaughan sideroad (Lot 21, Concession II) in 1855. The property was covered in white pine and had a stream running through it. Their first building was a sawmill and after the land had been cleared, they erected a foundry to produce their fanning mills, ploughshares and reapers. As business expanded, they added more buildings and houses for their workmen until their settlement became known as the village of Patterson. It had a Methodist church, a school and its own post office. The Pattersons were in the right business at the right time; in the five years between 1851 and 1856, the population

Patterson House (restored).
Collection of Mr. and Mrs. Ernest Redelmeier.

of Ontario had increased by 40% and agricultural exports had leaped ahead by the astronomical figure of 280%.[30] Demand for the Patterson's farm equipment was tremendous and orders came from as far as Wisconsin.

John and Lizzie's wedding in 1885 took place on one of those glorious September days which began, in the words of the *Richmond Hill Liberal,*

> as the bright and cheering sun rose above the eastern horizon in all its brilliancy... and penetrated the western sky with his beautiful rays... The residents of Patterson and vicinity awoke from their peaceful slumbers glad to find that such a desirable day had been chosen to celebrate the interesting event which was to take place that afternoon. Every accommodation was made to render the event one of enjoyment...

The wedding was held at the Patterson's house, which the *Liberal* described:

Drawing Room, Patterson House. c. 1880.
Collection of Mr. and Mrs. Ernest Redelmeier

The beautiful lawn surrounding the handsome residence, and which at all times presents a very tasty and cheerful appearance, never before looked so grand . . . On the west side of the lawn and close by a row of evergreen trees, a spacious and commodious tent, over 80 feet long, was substantially erected, the wooden framework being neatly covered with heavy canvas. At the south entrance a well-proportioned arch, the neatest and most accurate it has ever been our pleasure to witness, was built of cedar boughs. At the top of the arch and directly in the centre, was placed a keystone covered with maple leaves and on this placed a beautiful bouquet of wild autumn flowers. [31]

The bride was "attired with perfect taste in the richest cream satin with Duchess lace, orange blossoms and diamond ornaments" and attended by four bridesmaids. The guest list included Pattersons from the United States, some of whom came from as far away as California, and many Taylors. This was the third successive generation to have a link with Vaughan Township.

Although "Aunt Cook", John's daughter, and her husband were long dead, their three sons and their wives were present at the wedding. Other members of the family present were John F.'s father George and his step-mother, his married brothers and sisters, the Smiths, Hendersons, Taskers, and Davies; and along with their mother, Nancy Taylor, were his cousins John H. and Thomas and their sister Henrietta Pinkerton from Montreal. The Thomas Taylor branch of the family included the John Logans, the William Walmsleys, William Lewis and his unmarried sisters Florence and Kate. Elizabeth Morse's three sons and their wives were invited along with the Bright relations, the William Gooderhams, Mrs. Stegman and Fred Worts and business associates from the Bank of Commerce, W.H. Beatty, E.S. Cox, A.M. Crosby and Robert Kilgour. John F. Taylor's best man was Alderman Thomas Davies for whom he had been groomsman.

There was a "sumptuous dinner" and after the speeches, the bride and groom left for New York, Philadelphia, Baltimore and Washington in a private railway car. Lizzie's sister Susan, who was one of her bridesmaids, later went to New York on her honeymoon as well and it was the tragedy of the Patterson family that she died in a fire at the hotel in which she was staying.

John F. Taylor and Lizzie lived near his family in Doncaster, the village south of Todmorden on Broadview Avenue, on their return from the honeymoon and then moved to "Beechwood" until their new house to the west on Don Mills Road was built. [32] This handsome mansion, which they called "Fernwood Place", is now part of the United Church's Ina Grafton Gage Home for the Aged at 2 O'Connor Drive. There have been many additions and alterations to the house, but fortunately such details as the handsome woodwork and the colourful tiles around the fireplaces remain. Features of the house were the brilliant stained glass windows on the landing to the second floor and the stately front doors. John and Lizzie planned their house with great care.

A further note about the Pattersons should be added. Changes occurred in the family business which led to the disappearance of the village of Patterson and the loss of the importance of the family in Vaughan. The firm decided to expand in the same year as Lizzie's wedding and asked the Richmond Hill Council for

Fernwood Place, 2 O'Connor Drive.
Todmorden Mills Archives

assistance in financing the construction of a spur of the Northern Railway to its plant. The local council delayed and when it finally decided to make a small offer, it was too little and too late. The Pattersons had accepted the proposal of the town of Woodstock where they were already excellent railway connections and an additional bonus of $35,000. The Pattersons left Vaughan in 1886 and without their business the village lost its purpose and faded away. The firm itself merged with Massey Harris in 1891 and its founder, Peter Patterson, died after a fall from a ladder in 1904.

The second son of George Taylor, George Arthur, was also a member of the new firm of Taylor Brothers. He was twenty-eight when the partnership was formed in 1880, but only a brief word about him need be made. He was the victim of an unfortunate accident; it was said that a long scarf he was wearing got caught in the huge paper rollers in one of the mills and, to save himself from being drawn into the machinery, he pulled backwards with such force that he suffered permanent brain damage. He never married, although it was said that he was once engaged to Fidelia Davies, one of the daughters of Thomas Davies. He spent the rest of his life in Todmorden cared for by various members of the Taylor family.

Notes

1. Victor Ross, *History of the Canadian Bank of Commerce* (Toronto: Oxford University Press, 1920, 1922), 2 vols.; A. St. L. Trigge, *History of the Canadian Bank of Commerce*, Volume 3 (Toronto: Canadian Bank of Commerce, 1934), v. 2, p. 9.
2. *Ibid.*, p. 19.
3. *Dictionary of Canadian Biography* (Toronto: University of Toronto Press), v. X, p. 672.
4. Ross and Trigge, v. 2, p. 20.
5. *Ibid.*, p. 24.
6. L.B. Martyn, *100 Years of Grandeur* (Toronto: Pagurian Press, 1978), p. 130.
7. C.T. Currelly, *I Brought the Ages Home* (Toronto: Ryerson Press, 1956), p. 224.
8. *Dictionary of Canadian Biography*, v. X, p. 131.
9. R.O. #2036R, Probate 12 August 1871.
10. *The Star*, undated, from family scrapbook.
11. J.A. Blyth, "The Development of the Paper Industry in Old Ontario, 1824 - 1867", in *Ontario History*, v. LXII, 1970, p. 131.
12. *Ibid.*, p. 282.
13. J. Temperlake, *Illustrated Toronto, Past and Present* (Toronto: Peter A. Gross, 1877), p. 282.
14. George Carruthers, *Paper in the Making* (New Jersey: Garden City Press, 1947), p. 312.
15. *Ibid.*, p. 316.
16. *Ibid.*, p. 317.
17. Ross Wallace, "Eighty Score Years and Twelve", (Orillia, unpublished, 1973), genealogy of the Thomas Taylor family, p. 19.
18. A.S. Thompson, *Jarvis Street* (Toronto: Personal Library, 1980), p. 162.
19. C.P. Mulvany, *Toronto Past and Present*, (Toronto: W.E. Caiger, 1884, Ontario Reprint Press, 1970), p. 43.
20. Ross Wallace, p. 19.

21. *Ibid.,* p. 23.
22. Elizabeth Axon, "Some Memories of Old Don Mills Road", *The Globe and Mail,* June 4, 1955.
23. The date was June 30, 1880.
24. R.O. #GR203, Probate August 12, 1871, registered September 2, 1874.
25. R.O. #13013, February 6, 1880; see Plan of Subdivision of John Taylor's estate prepared by Peter Gibson.
26. R.O. #17836, April 8, 1885, and R.O. #28045, June 14, 1888.
27. R.O. #28088, January 8, 1888.
28. *Toronto Directory,* 1890, p. 1238.
29. Commemorative Biographical Record of the County of York, (Toronto: J.H. Beers Co., 1907), Thomas Bright Taylor, p. 480.
30. Gail Crawford, "Patterson" in *The York Pioneer,* 1976, p. 210.
31. (RHPL), "An Interesting Event" in *The Liberal* (Richmond Hill), September 24, 1885.
32. *Toronto Directory,* 1885, p. 733.

William Thomas Taylor, 1857-1944.
Author's collection

VI

WILLIAM THOMAS TAYLOR
AND THE
DON VALLEY PRESSED BRICK WORKS

The youngest brother in the family partnership of Taylor Brothers was William Thomas Taylor, who was twenty-three when his father George and his uncle Thomas retired in 1880. The 1871 Census described him as a "paper maker" although he was only thirteen and could hardly have finished his education at the Model School at the time. Two interesting reminders of the sort of education he received are a small framed slate on which he wrote and his sketchbook containing meticulous drawings of animals, birds and buildings. As future boss of the Taylor paper mills, he started his training at an early age and like the rest of the family had only a limited formal education.

A tall, spare, handsome man, with a quiet nature, he did not marry the domineering Isabella McLellan, who he always said was "little but mighty", until he was twenty-seven. She was three months older and considered a beauty, one of the belles of Toronto who never forgot the gaiety of the parties she had once attended in the great houses that lined Jarvis Street. She and "Will", as she called him, were married at noon in Bloor Street Presbyterian Church in October 1884 and went to New York for their honeymoon. [1]

Isabella's family, the McLellans, were part of the early history of York. Malcolm, her grandfather, was a tailor who had been ordained as an elder in the Secessionist Presbyterian Church in 1827. In Edith Firth's *The Town of York, 1815 – 1834*, he was severely criticised along with another elder, Edward Henderson, by the Rev. William Proudfoot for admitting "even Methodists to the fellowship of the Church" and permitting "at least one" to "be at the Lord's Table". Proudfoot condemned this as "carrying free communion with a vengeance". [2]

Isabella McLellan Taylor, 1857-1951. This photograph was taken when she was sixteen and won a gold medal at an international exhibition in Paris. Photographer unknown.
Author's collection

Isabella's father James died from pneumonia after fighting a fire in York as a volunteer fireman. Her mother Elizabeth Sleeth was considered too young (she was nineteen) by her husband's sisters to look after her infant daughter. These aunts brought up Isabella in a house on the site of the former Carlton Street United Church near Yonge Street, where, in accordance with their Presbyterian upbringing, each Sunday the curtains were drawn and the day was observed in oppressive gloom. After her mother remarried, Isabella went to live with her and her stepfather John Shaw, whom she adored. His eccentricities and colourful personality made him a delightful part of the Taylor family, and no account of the Taylors would be complete without reference to him.

Like the McLellans, the Shaws were members of the working class in York. John's father, George, was a Scottish immigrant and builder who had arrived in 1832, married Laura Jackson and had five sons—Robert, John William, George, Albert—and one daughter, Susan. [3] John was born in 1837 and because of his ability was sent to Upper Canada College and Victoria College before studying law and becoming a barrister in 1870. In 1884, he began his long career in civic politics by being elected Alderman for St. Paul's Ward. By the time he became Mayor in 1897, he had served as Chairman of both the Fire and Light Commission and the Works Commission, and had been delegated to negotiate the sale of Toronto City bonds in England. He also knew how to endear himself to the voters. In 1895, for instance, when the encumbent Mayor, Warring Kennedy, was absent in England, Shaw coped with a major crisis as President of the Council. When the water pipes in the Bay rose to the surface, the supply of drinking water for the city was cut off. Undaunted, he immediately arranged for water casks to be delivered to every house in the city for six weeks until the pipes were repaired.

During the two terms that he served as Mayor, from 1897 to 1899, he was anxious to maintain the city's position as the province's commercial centre and appointed the Toronto-Hudson Bay Railway Commission to investigate the feasibility of the city building its own railway to James Bay. In theory it sounded very impressive until one considers what products James Bay would have to offer to the markets of Toronto. A surveyor was sent north in the spring and Shaw himself followed

John Shaw, 1837-1917.
Author's collection

in the summer and stayed at the Matabunik Hotel in Haileybury where he reported that his expenses for twenty-nine meals and a flask of whiskey amounted to $10.30. [4] The railway proved too ambitious for the city to undertake on its own, but the efforts of the Commission spurred the province to build the Temiskaming and Northern Railway which in time became the well-known Ontario Northland Railway.

Toronto City Hall c. 1875, corner of Front and Jarvis Streets.
Ontario Archives

Instead, the city politicians had to content themselves with local matters and decide that it was time to finish the city hall. The old building, where Shaw had the distinction of serving as the last Mayor, had been built in 1844 at a cost of $45,000. It was a picturesque structure originally at the edge of the Bay, with shops on either side of the government block, and behind it were vegetable and fruit markets. A picture of the Council Chamber reveals its Victorian splendour, with draperies and flowing glass curtains suspended from massive rods, portraits of former mayors on the walls, and the whole dominated by a large painting

Toronto City Hall, completed 1899. Corner of Queen and Bay Streets.
Metropolitan Toronto Public Library

of the young Queen Victoria and a marble bust of the Prince Consort. [5] The remains of this building are still visible in the St. Lawrence Market.

As early as 1885, the city had decided that it needed a new Court House and fifty architects submitted designs in a international competition. Nothing came of this because the cost of the building far exceeded the budget. But the following year another competition was held with thirteen architects presenting plans and J.E. Lennox won. [6] According to Eric Arthur in his book *Toronto, No Mean City*, the cost again affected the con-

John Shaw, the politician.
Author's collection

struction and the excavation for the foundation remained a large hole and was used as a skating rink in the winter. However, in 1887, the Council decided that a new City Hall was also needed and Lennox was asked to submit drawings to combine the two. Arthur calls the city hall the "best known and best loved building in Toronto", but in 1899 the city fathers were still waiting for it to be finished. During a particularly vocal meeting of Council, Shaw decided to do something about it and with his characteristic flair picked up his mayor's chair and, carrying it before him, marched along Queen Street followed by the delighted members of his Council to the new building. Once there, he set down his chair in the middle of the wood shavings and to the consternation of the workmen called the meeting to order. [8]

On the opening of the new building on September 18, 1899, Shaw was presented with a gold key which he later gave to the Royal Ontario Museum. His wife Lizzie borrowed her daughter's jewellery for the occasion. (When Isabella married William Taylor, he gave her gold jewellery set with pearls and diamonds.) But at the last moment Mrs. Shaw decided to wear only the heavy gold locket and chain and left the matching earrings, bracelet and brooch at home. Thieves broke into the Shaw house during the ceremony and the jewellery was stolen.

That day Shaw made a splendid speech, part of which Eric Arthur quotes:

> *Why people will spend large sums of money on great buildings opens up a wide field of thought. It may, however, be roughly answered that great buildings symbolize a people's deeds and aspirations. It has been said that, wherever a nation had a conscience and a mind, it recorded the evidence of its being in the highest products of this greatest of all arts. Where no such monuments are to be found, the mental and moral nature of the people have not been above the faculties of the beasts.* [9]

Arthur adds that "after such a statement, few had the temerity to put themselves on the moral level of beasts" and question the massive cost of $2,500,000 in the days when the annual city budget was only $300,000. [10] It was such a moving address that one of the aldermen, John Hallam, burst into tears and Shaw was forced to stop and ask for him to be taken out. This digression and display of emotion led Shaw to remind the audience of the preceding decade leading up to the opening day—city hall fights, public plebescites over rising costs, contractor scandals, issues which have a familiar ring today. [11]

John and Lizzie Shaw in front of the Shaw Cottage, Bloor Street near Avenue Road.
Author's collection

    John and Lizzie Shaw lived in "Shaw Cottage", a house that he bought from his aunt Mrs. Kendrick in 1877. This house was originally built in 1818 [12] and was located just west of Avenue Road on Bloor Street on land that once belonged to William Baldwin of "Mashquoteh" before he donated it to the Church of The Redeemer as a contribution to its endowment. It was called "an old time forest residence", built when the area south of Bloor Street was still heavily forested and there were only half a dozen houses between it and Dundas Street. Bloor Street, it will be remembered, was named after Joseph Bloor, who ran a brewery at the bottom of the ravine at the north end of Huntley Street and who was a partner with Sheriff Jarvis in the speculative development of the village of Yorkville. [13]

    The Shaws entertained frequently when John was mayor and the grounds surrounding the cottage were noted for their flower gardens, climbing plants, shrubs, fruit and shade trees. When the Shaws gave a birthday party for their grand-daughter, the author's mother Beatrice Taylor, the band of the 48th Highlanders played music and the trees were strung with lighted Japanese lanterns in the evening.

    John Shaw adored children and it was great sorrow to him

that he and Lizzie had none of their own. However, one day a woman came to his office with her daughter, an adorable three-year-old with dark curly hair. She sat on his knee while the mother told the mayor of her hard luck and begged him to look after the child. He was so captivated by the little girl and so sympathetic to the mother's story that he agreed and took her home. The child's name was Mabel and John and Lizzie adopted her, but unwisely decided not to tell her that she was adopted until she was eighteen. When she eventually found out, she ran away from home and ended up in Chicago where she married Charles Crane and had four children. She died in 1921 and her youngest son "Frankie" was sent to Toronto for Mrs. Shaw to look after. She was much too old to care for him and he was sent to live with her daughter Isabella until he too was adopted by a Toronto family.

Isabella's children always spoke fondly of "Johnny" as they called Shaw. They remembered him coming to visit their house "Bellehaven" in Todmorden, wearing a dapper pale summer suit with a flower in the lapel, his blue eyes twinkling as he thanked the workman who had given him a lift in his cart. He was a true politician and always had the happy gift of being a friend to all. When he had finished his visit and was ready to return to the city, he often chose one of the five children to accompany him—a coveted honour. The child was allowed to go with him on the street car as far as the Albany Club on King Street where he got out and paid the driver to take the child back.

Shaw was a Greek scholar and an authority on Shakespeare, whom he loved to quote, but there was a black side to him as well. He was addicted to gambling at very high stakes and an entire row of houses could be lost at a throw of dice. He also went on massive drinking bouts and had to be hospitalized with delirium tremens, a malady causing terrifying delusions. He gave up municipal politics in 1899, but in 1908 was elected to the Ontario Legislature for North Toronto. However, he resigned for unknown reasons shortly after his election. He died in 1917, when he was eighty and the funeral held at St. Paul's Church on Bloor Street was a fitting tribute to one who had been one of Toronto's best known citizens. When his will was probated, *The Globe and Mail* reported that John Shaw left the modest estate of

William and Isabella Taylor on their honeymoon in New York, 1884.
Author's collection

$22,056.[14] Isabella was bequeathed a legacy of $300 and each of her five children received $100. Mabel was given $250 and her three children Murray, Elizabeth and Madeline Crane received $50 each. "Frankie" was not born at the time.

William and Isabella Taylor spent the first three years of their marriage in John Eastwood's stone house at the foot of Pottery Road hill where their second child, a son, died. This house had been built in 1832 and eventually burned down about 1935. Edna Ash, who lived there as a child when her father was

Bellehaven, residence of W.T. Taylor, 1068 Broadview Avenue, demolished in the 1950s.
Author's collection

the manager of the Lower and Middle Mills, described it: "The ground floor contained the customary living-rooms and a ballroom and behind the dining room a cold pantry with hooks presumably for hanging wild game. The second floor had five bedrooms, a nursery and a bathroom." It was a stone house with wide window sills and green shutters outside, but the Taylors found that living in the valley was too damp and they decided to build a new house at the top of the hill. This they gave the Victorian name of "Bellehaven", inspired by Isabella who was often called "Belle". It was an imposing mansion reported to have been made from 75,000 bricks made in a private kiln near one of the Taylor paper plants and had nineteen rooms, nine fireplaces, a conservatory, large halls and magnificent stained-glass windows. The most spectacular window was on the north side of the house, lighting the stairs from the second to the third floors and portraying three knights in armour on their horses— one white, one brown and one black. No expense was spared. The tiles around the fireplaces were hand-painted with scenes of the lochs and were imported from Scotland. In the dining room a specially designed massive oak cupboard resplendent with

The North Parlour, Bellehaven.
Author's collection

The Dining Room, Bellehaven.
Author's collection

The Taylor children and their friends in 1899 where the old willow tree used to stand.
Author's collection

mirrors, plate glass and carvings filled one wall. Throughout the main floor, there was dark, carved woodwork, oriental rugs covered the floors and the dark wood furniture in the north and south parlors was upholstered in the drab olive green and deep red plush that the Victorians loved. In the halls were stuffed deer's heads that William had shot, and the smoking room or office beside the north entrance was a cosy room with a large oak roll-top desk and cases of stuffed birds. Upstairs, enormous wardrobes served as cupboards and on the third floor were pine boxes as long as coffins where furs were stored in camphor during the summer months.

In time, William and Isabella's five children—three girls and two boys—had a playroom on the third floor. This became the billiard room when the children outgrew the nursery. The basement was cavernous and had storage rooms for apples and tools and a room with a wood stove where the cook helped Mrs. Taylor make the Christmas puddings she gave as presents each year. It was a lively household with Mrs. Ensminger coming to do the laundry and her husband Tom helping to look after the horses and gardens. There were Irish maids who came and

Beatrice and Carrie Taylor c. 1915.
Author's collection

went, a cook called "old Anne" who played the piano divinely, accompanied by a hound who howled in chorus to her music, and "Granny" Arnold, who came first as a nursemaid and who reappeared to help whenever she needed a place to live.

    The girls, Edna, Beatrice and Carrie, were sent to Branksome Hall for a time, but William did not believe in too much education and thought daughters should remain at home until they married. Edna was one of the first pupils at Branksome Hall when the school was started on Bloor Street and she and her sister Beatrice revered Miss Scott, the first Principal. Carrie's most vivid recollection of her schooldays was having her hand crushed in a teeter-totter and being put to bed in the room of Miss Read, who

Leland and George, William Taylor's sons.
Author's collection

succeeded Miss Scott as Principal. The honour was doubly impressive because she was also given a glass of sherry to revive her. Isabella's favourite son George was sent to St. Andrew's College, but his brother Leland attended Riverdale Collegiate, since by 1910 the family's circumstances had substantially altered.

Although the Taylors had long operated paper mills and had added a few other products to their business, in about 1890 they started an important new venture—the Don Valley Pressed Brick Works. Although the plant, until recently the Toronto Brick Company, continued in operation until 1984 on the same site west of the Bayview Avenue Extension and north of Bloor

Street, there are no early records available. William Taylor was considered to be its founder and we have to rely on the story his son Leland told Charles Sauriol in the 1940s.

> *In April of 1882 . . . at that time the area was dotted with meadows and the valley walls were covered with trees. It so happened that in the month of April, 1882, Mr. Wm. T. Taylor and a helper were erecting a fence. Mr. Taylor paused from time to time to examine the cores of clay which the post hole digger or its equivalent had brought to the surface. He thought that the clay was of unusually fine texture, and a curious discussion ensued between the two men as to the value of the clay for brick-making. To settle the discussion, Mr. Taylor returned to the scene the next day with two small cigar boxes which he proceeded to fill with clay. He then sauntered down the valley to a small brick works then in operation near the present Bloor Street Viaduct. A lively argument sprang up between the owner of the kiln and Mr. Taylor who insisted that the samples of clay would bake red. "You're wrong", the brickmaker replied, "They'll bake grey". "That stuff is only ordinary brick clay . . ."*
>
> *A few days later Mr. Taylor returned to the kiln and according to the story as it was told to me by the late Leland Taylor, he found ready for him several samples of bricks baked to a beautiful shade of cherry red. The owner of the kiln admitted that they were two of the best sample bricks he had ever seen. "If the entire seam is like those samples", he said to William Taylor, "Then you have a gold mine lying in that bend on the Don Valley". Gold mine or clay pit, William Taylor conveyed the details of his find to his brothers John and George, whereupon the three men decided after considerable testing of the clay seam, to establish their own brick manufacturing plant in the Don Valley.* [15]

Brickmaking in Toronto had had a slow start even though Governor Simcoe had proposed opening a brickyard near the Garrison in 1792. The bricks first used in Toronto were said to have been made in the village of Yorkville. Bricks were burned to order by itinerant brickmakers who set up kilns close to the

The Don Valley Brick Works, 1893.
Author's collection

construction site. It was not until 1825 that permanent brickyards were opened and brickmaking became a business rather than a trade. By 1840, there were brickyards in the lower valley and by 1850 there were several others in the Yorkville area. They turned out the familiar yellowish-white bricks that were used in buildings north of College Street. [16] The Monteith brickyard was the earliest in the Don Valley. It was established by 1818 at the mouth of the Don River. [17] Farther up the river, families like the Playters and Leas made their own bricks, and there had been small quarries located off Pottery Road and at the foot of Beechwood Drive. William Lea thought that the Eastwoods and Helliwells had made their own bricks for the brewery and distillery about 1820. [18]

In 1866, only two brick manufacturers, Nightingale and Thomas, near Yorkville, and James Morin, on the Kingston Road, were listed, but by 1880, twelve were noted. Taylor Brothers were included for the first time in 1889 and the following year there were thirty-two firms listed in the *Toronto Directory* as brick manufacturers. This increase reflected the huge increase in population and industrial development. The city had grown by absorbing the surrounding suburban villages, four new wards were created, and in the period from 1879 to 1889, the assessable property in the city had increased from about fifty million dollars to over one hundred and thirty-six million dollars. [19]

It was reported in the *First Annual Report* of the Department of Mines that the Don Valley Pressed Brick Works was erected in the early part of 1891 and that the plant was fitted with "the best and most modern equipment". [20] This consisted of four power presses with a capacity of 44,000 bricks and grinding and screening machinery in which the clay was prepared for the presses. Several buildings and eight kilns had been erected at the time of the report. Fifty men, exclusive of teamsters, were employed in the quarries and works. It was also noted that while the business was barely established, there was a "fair prospect" of making shipments to Buffalo and other American cities.

The Taylors first blasted a quarry to the east of the present quarry, and all the work was done manually. Men shovelled the clay into carts which were pulled by horses or mules on a small track to the plant. There the clay was dumped and shovelled into the grinding and screening machines. Brickmaking today uses basically the same methods employed by the Taylors. Bricks were made by three methods: the soft-mud process which used considerable amounts of water; the dry-press method where the brick was formed in wooden or gypsum moulds and only 10% water was mixed with the clay; and the stiff-mud process which used a mixture of 18% water after which the clay was formed into long columns from which the bricks were cut. The colour of the brick depended on the chemical content of the clay. More limestone produced a buff colour, manganese turned them brown and iron oxide produced various shades of red. The wood or coal burning kilns required from four days to three weeks to fire the bricks compared to the two-day cycle in the scientifically controlled gas kilns of today. After the bricks were cooled they were unloaded and stacked manually. When two bricks were knocked together they produced a strong ringing tone which Mr. Albert Huber, the last manager and brickmaker of the plant, said was the mark of a good brick. When the bricks were shipped, it took a team of four horses to haul the load of 1,000 bricks weighing three tons up the Pottery Road hill. The Taylors kept a large stable of more than 400 horses and mules at the brickyard and there were additional stables and a hayloft at the bottom of the hill. Later, shipments were considerably facilitated by the railway siding at the plant.

By 1892, the Taylor firm was well established and offered a

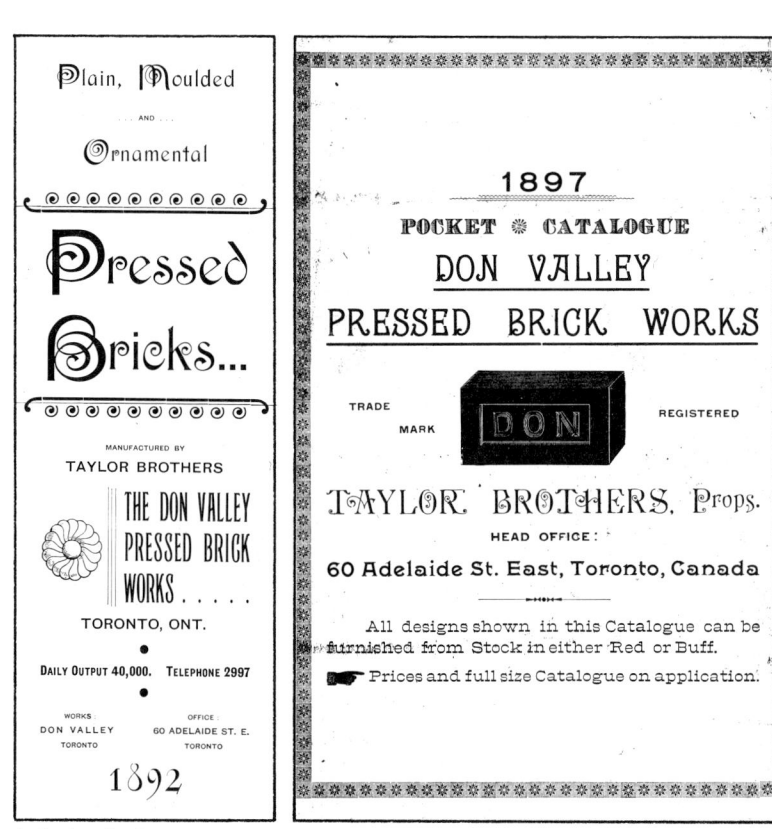

Author's collection

Collection of Ronald R. Tasker

Workman's House, Pottery Road, photographed in 1920s.
Todmorden Mills Archives

broad range of products to "architects and patrons", both "plain moulded and ornamental pressed bricks".[21] The slim red leather catalogue stated that letters had been received from leading architects in Canada and the United States acknowledging the high quality of the bricks. Indeed, a letter from Col. E.E. Meyers, an architect in Detroit, stated that he had never seen such "elegant bricks" in all his travels. There were ten shades of red brick and seven shades of buff, as well as ornamental bricks with moulded edges and thirty-six designs of "radious" bricks in all sizes. Terra cotta ridges, finials, panels, arches, chimneys, string courses, tiles and more could all be made to architect's specifications. Arrangements had also been made with Hamilton McCarthy, R.C.A., to "execute designs in Art Terra Cotta for exterior and interior decoration". As a young man, Walter Allward, the designer of the Boer War Monument on University Avenue in Toronto and the Vimy Ridge Memorial in France, was employed there and gave Mr. Taylor a charming panel of water babies that he had designed.

Furthermore, the firm boasted that it was the owner of the "only arch-grinding machine in Canada" and could supply arches to order on a few days notice. In 1892, the company was making 40,000 bricks per day and two years later it had increased its output to 114,000 bricks per day. The company shipped its wares to almost every point in Canada from St. John to Vancouver and to American cities such as Chicago and Detroit. In 1894, the firm won a gold medal at the Toronto Industrial Fair and a photograph of its display featured an ornate terra cotta urn. An engraving of the Don Valley Works was prepared by the Taylor's brother-in-law, David Smith, an engraver with the firm of Rolph, Smith and Company. John F. Taylor managed the entire business from the office at 60 Adelaide Street W. [22]

With the huge outlay of capital and innovative practices, the firm prospered since architects were designing city buildings constructed of brick with terra cotta decorations. Unfortunately, by 1896 a depression had set in which seriously affected the building trades and particularly the owners of quarries. The demand for bricks steadily declined and did not revive until after the turn of the century. It was disastrous for the Taylors and the brickyards passed into other hands. Bricks from the Taylor yards continued to be used in many of Toronto's important buildings including Casa Loma, the City Hall, Toronto General Hospital, the University of Toronto and many provincial government buildings, but these were produced by different owners.

There is an additional feature of the brickyards which would have surprised the Taylors. The quarry itself became world famous as new excavations exposed the entire glacial sequence of the Toronto area. Previously, the valley had been of interest to scientists because of the fossilized freshwater shells and trees imbedded twenty to thirty feet below the surface. Two early naturalists, Dr. William Brodie and J. Townsend, studied the drift deposits and identified a new species of maple called "Penhallow acer pleistocenium", the Pleistocene maple. More fossils were uncovered when the former Riverdale Zoo was being excavated by the prisoners from the nearby Don Jail and when the Belt Line Railway was constructed. But once the quarry had been started, it became of paramount importance to scientists. Like the Scarborough Bluffs to the east of the city, the quarry gave collectors "the widest range of interglacial fossils", and more importantly, "disclosed the relations of different beds to one another so that the history of the Pleistocene in southern Ontario could be worked out with certainty". [23] Dr. A.P. Coleman, Director of Geology at the Royal Ontario Museum and Dean of

Taylor Brothers' prize winning display at the Toronto Industrial Fair, 1894.
Author's collection

Arts at the University of Toronto, kept a record of developments and took members of the British Association for the Advancement of Science and a group of specialists in Pleistocene geology from the International Geological Congress to see what he called this "unsurpassed section of drift" when they met in Toronto in 1913. Work at the brickworks has been continuous over the years and there has been a constant stream of visitors, but the quarry has become rather dangerous and geologists now prefer to go to the more accessible Scarborough Bluffs for their teaching fieldtrips.

None of this would have come about without William Taylor's inspiration. It was such an important discovery that the manufacture of bricks continued for nearly a century on this site. However, it ruined the firm of Taylor Brothers. During the years of growth and prosperity, the family circle opened to encompass another family, the Davies, who, like the Helliwells and Brights, became intimately connected with the Taylors in the Don Valley. Unlike the other happy associations, however, this new connection proved to have disastrous consequences.

Notes

1. Wedding Announcement, "Taylor-McLellan", family scrapbook, n.d.
2. Edith Firth, *The Town of York: 1815 – 1834* (Toronto: University of Toronto Press, 1962), pp. 128, 217.
3. J.E. Middleton, *Municipality of York, A History* (Toronto: The Dominion Publishing Company, 1923), 3 vols., v. III, p. 101.
4. *The Globe and Mail*, "Northern Vision and John Shaw", 1961, author's collection.
5. *Evening Telegram*, "Do You Remember Back When?", n.d., author's collection.
6. Eric Arthur, *Toronto, No Mean City* (Toronto: University of Toronto Press, 1964), pp. 204-205.
7. *Ibid.*, pp. 205-206.
8. *The Globe and Mail*, "They Took the City Hall by Storm", June 1, 1957.
9. Eric Arthur, p. 205.
10. *Ibid.*, p. 205.
11. *The Toronto Star*, "September 18, 1899: The Last Time We Opened a New City Hall", September 4, 1963.
12. John Ross Robertson, *Landmarks of Toronto* (Toronto: Toronto Evening Telegram, 1898), 6 vols., v. III, p. 272.
13. Eric Arthur, p. 56.
14. *The Globe and Mail*, February 19, 1918.
15. Charles Sauriol, *Remembering the Don* (Toronto: Consolidated Amethyst Communications Inc., 1981), p. 127.
16. Department of Planning and Development, Don Valley Conservation Report, 1950, p. 161.
17. (TMA), Map of York, 1797-1818.
18. (TMA), J. Remple, "The Family of John Lea and the History of Leaside", Remple Papers.
19. G. Mercer Adam, *Toronto Old and New* (Toronto: The Mail Printing Co., 1891), p. 154.
20. (Metropolitan Toronto Public Library), Department of Mines, *Annual Report*, 1899.

21. *Don Valley Pressed Works, Pocket Catalogue, 1892* (author's collection).
22. *Ibid.*
23. A.P. Coleman, *The Pleistocene of the Toronto Region* (Ottawa: Department of Mines, 1932), part vii, pp. 5-7.

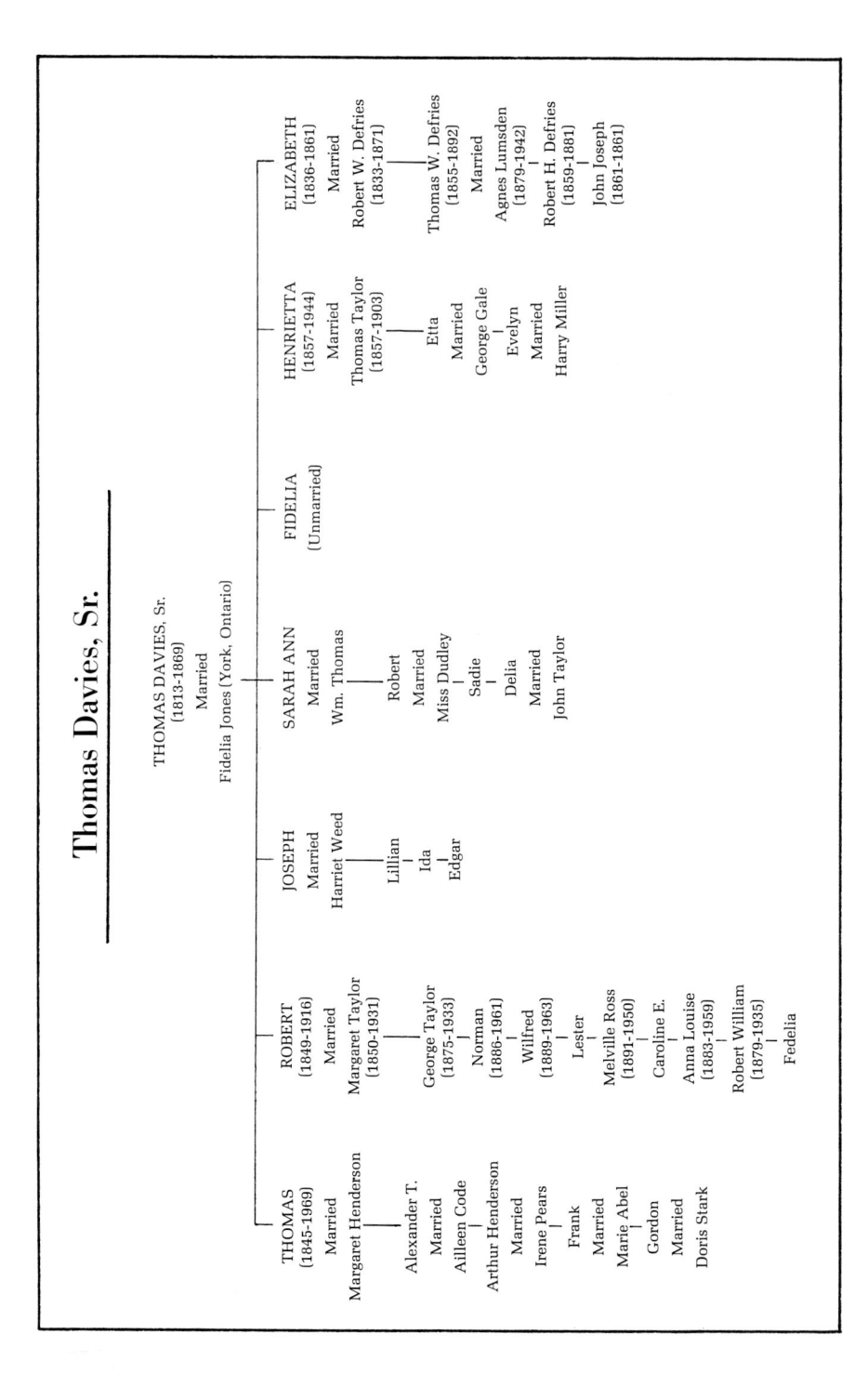

Thomas Davies, Sr.

THOMAS DAVIES, Sr.
(1813-1869)
Married
Fidelia Jones (York, Ontario)

THOMAS
(1845-1969)
Married
Margaret Henderson

- Alexander T.
- Ailleen Code
  Married
  Arthur Henderson
- Irene Pears
  Married
  Frank
- Marie Abel
  Married
  Gordon
- Doris Stark
  Married

ROBERT
(1849-1916)
Married
Margaret Taylor
(1850-1931)

- George Taylor
  (1875-1933)
- Norman
  (1886-1961)
- Wilfred
  (1889-1963)
- Lester
- Melville Ross
  (1891-1950)
- Caroline E.
- Anna Louise
  (1883-1959)
- Robert William
  (1879-1935)
- Fedelia

JOSEPH
Married
Harriet Weed

- Lillian
- Ida
- Edgar

SARAH ANN
Married
Wm. Thomas

- Robert
  Married
  Miss Dudley
- Sadie
- Delia
  Married
  John Taylor

FIDELIA
(Unmarried)

HENRIETTA
(1857-1944)
Married
Thomas Taylor
(1857-1903)

- Etta
  Married
  George Gale
- Evelyn
  Married
  Harry Miller

ELIZABETH
(1836-1861)
Married
Robert W. Defries
(1833-1871)

- Thomas W. Defries
  (1855-1892)
  Married
  Agnes Lumsden
  (1879-1942)
- Robert H. Defries
  (1859-1881)
- John Joseph
  (1861-1861)

VII

THE DAVIES

The Taylors had known the Davies family for many years. Their relationship had been strengthened by two marriages in the 1880s, a rumoured engagement and various close friendships. The first generation of each family had emigrated from England to York and pioneered as farmers before they became manufacturers—the Taylors with their mills in the middle part of the Don Valley and the Davies with breweries centered around Queen and River Streets. Both prospered and by the end of the century they had formed close business relationships and even had connections in municipal politics. Some members of both families had moved to Toronto, but most still lived on River Street and in Todmorden. Because they were so closely associated, the history of the Taylors is not complete without an account of the Davies.

Thomas Davies emigrated from Cheshire, England in 1832, sailing on the same ship as William Gooderham, who was travelling with his fourteen children and forty other relatives. [1] Gooderham founded a distillery and built the well-known windmill at the east end of Toronto harbour. Davies became a brewer farther up the Don River. Before this, Davies tried his hand at farming on land between Yonge Street and Bayview Avenue, just north of what became Mount Pleasant Cemetery (Lot 18, Concession I). It was here that he brought his pretty bride, Fidelia Jones, with whom he had eloped. Her father lived on Yonge Street, south of St. Clair Avenue, where Jackes Avenue commemorates the name of Samuel Jackes, one of the Jones' sons-in-law. The Davies had seven children: Thomas, Joseph, Robert, Sarah Ann, Elizabeth, Fidelia and Henrietta Victoria and when the brewery was started in 1849 they all moved to a house nearby at 33 River Street. [2]

Thomas Davies, Senior, 1813-1869.
Collection of George Taylor Gale

The Davies brewery prospered and in 1872 advertised that it operated at a capacity of 3,500 gallons of beer per day. [3] The three sons went into the family business, which changed its name from "Thomas Davies and Son" to "Thomas Davies and Brother", then to "Thomas Davies and Company" and finally to the "Davies Brewing and Malting Company". [4] However, the three brothers were not compatible, perhaps because of the youngest, Robert, who had a contentious nature and announced when he was only fourteen that one day he would own the

Fidelia Jones Davies.
Collection of George Taylor Gale

brewery. [5] He was educated at Upper Canada College and when he was twenty-three went into partnership with his brother Joseph in the Don Brewing Company, which lasted from 1873 until 1878. He then went into business for himself and began the Dominion Brewery at 412-468 Queen Street East. There he followed his father's axiom that "a man never died of hard work". [6] He aimed to "brew more and sell more" and "as many barrels as he brewed each day from early morning until evening, that many he sold by personal canvass before he went to bed". [7]

33 River Street, residence of Thomas Davies.
Collection of George Taylor Gale

By 1885, the *Toronto Directory* listed 13 breweries operating in the city and five of these were connected with the Davies family: the Ontario Brewing and Malting Company, the Copland Brewery, the Davies Brewing and Malting Company, the Dominion Brewery, and the East End Brewery (later the Reinhardt Brewery). The husbands of three of Davies' daughters became brewers as well and, in the next generation, Robert's daughter Caroline married Lothar Reinhardt, the son of a brewmaster whom her father had brought out from Germany to work at the Dominion Brewery. When Lothar's father started his own brewery, Davies was so displeased with his daughter's marriage that he left her only a nominal amount in his will. She apparently had the same contentious nature as her father and contested the will in court. [8]

Thomas Davies' daughter Sarah Ann married William John Thomas in 1876. He was the owner of the Queen City Malting Company, which became the Ontario Brewing and Malting Company in 1889, and was located at the corner of Ontario and

Thomas Davies and Brothers, Maltsters, Brewers and Bottlers.
Toronto Illustrated, Past and Present

King Streets. He eventually became the president of the Davies Brewing and Malting Company and was highly regarded for his executive ability. [9] Since he started his career as an architect, the family has often confused him with the well-known Toronto architect of the same name. [10] The other William John Thomas, who is best known as the designer of Brock's monument at Niagara, worked in Toronto earlier in the century and also had offices in Lower Canada and Nova Scotia. [11]

Another son-in-law who came from a brewing family was Robert William Defries who married Elizabeth Davies. The Defries family, like the Davies, have a street named after them in the area of River and Queen Streets and their East End Brewery was situated higher up the river. It was built by Robert Defries, an Englishman who came to York in 1829 and served as Postmaster of the House of Assembly for thirty-six years (1835-1871). [12] When he died, he stipulated in his will that no Davies would ever be associated with his brewery and it was left to his two younger sons rather than to Elizabeth's husband. The rivalry between the two grandfathers, however, did not continue into the next generation. Elizabeth's son, William Thomas Defries, worked in the office of the Dominion Brewery until he died at the age of thirty-eight. However, his widow, who was very devout, would have no part of the brewing business for her sons

The Davies Brewery, a later view.
Toronto Illustrated, Past and Present

and was determined that they should attend university. Both graduated in medicine and one of them later attributed this to "her simple faith in God and the power of prayer". Others attributed it to the generosity of their uncle Robert Davies. [13]

The process of making beer varied little from brewery to brewery. Some, like the Davies, used city water while others, such as the Coplands, claimed that spring water made all the difference. From October to June, the Davies made their own malt from barley. The grain was first elevated to a loft at the malt house and poured down into large tubs of water in order to soak. The water was then drained off and the wet grain was spread across the malting floor where it was turned and tended night and day to encourage germination. This converted the starches in the grain into soluble sugars. After this it was dried in the two kilns the Davies kept constantly fired as part of their extensive malting department. It was then loaded into malt chambers where it was weighed by an excise officer and after a tax of 36¢ per bushel was paid, it was released to be brewed.

Winter on the Don River.
Ontario Archives

Winter was the busiest time for brewing. The malt was screened and ground between large iron rollers before it was mixed with almost boiling water and passed into malt tubs. The liquor or "wort" from this was then boiled and hops were added to give it flavour. The Davies imported their hop blossoms, costing between fifteen and forty cents per pound, from England and Bavaria. These came in two hundred-pound bales and were a heavy item of expense. The liquid had to be cooled before it was run into 125 gallon kegs for fermentation. Good beer, then as now, called for the human touch and it was up to the brewmaster to taste and decide when it was ready. If he had an off day, the quality of the beer suffered. [14]

In 1877, the Davies Brewery was described as "fitted up with great ingenuity" so that the various departments functioned with "fewer hands than anywhere in Canada", [15] and the Davies brothers were proud to announce that "more business is done in proportion to the number of hands employed than in any other establishment of its kind in the Dominion". [16] They were one of the first to have a system of forcing water to the highest level without using pumps, and this was copied by others. Another feature was the bottling department where machinery rinsed, drained, bottled, corked and tin-foiled with great efficiency and

The Don River.
Ontario Archives

their imported corking machine was "much admired". [17] Thousands of bottles of ale and porter were arranged on shelves in an adjoining room, waiting to be sold.

Thomas Davies Jr., who took over from his father at the brewery, was better known as Alderman Davies. He was active in municipal politics for over forty years and was a contemporary of John Shaw, but, although he ran in 1909 and 1913, he was never elected mayor. [18] He was influential in having the city streets and sidewalks paved, the naming of High Park and Riverdale Park, and he was one of the originators of the Board of Control. [19] He was also one of the chief promoters of a controversial plan to straighten the Don River after a major flood occurred on September 14, 1878. On that day, the river rose to an unprecedented height of more than eight feet. The resulting destruction was witnessed by John J. Burgess, who had been an employee of the Taylors for most of his life. He never forgot that day:

> I remember standing on the hill... and looking down on the waters rolling down towards the lake. I saw the flood pick up the river bridge like a straw is picked up in a gutter in a heavy rainstorm and carried away.... All the dams went out and the bridges too. The paper mills were flooded. Cattle went out on the waters...[20]

To prevent a recurrence, it was decided to eliminate the big bend in the river which curved east from the Winchester Bridge to Broadview Avenue across the flats to the west of Riverdale Park near Geneva Street. Some of Scadding's land was expropriated, the high-level, half-mile railway bridge was built and the islands and the wild rice in the river were submerged. The project was completed in 1888, but not without a great deal of controversy over land expropriation and the right of way of the railways.

Thomas Davies Jr. and his family of four sons lived at "Rivervilla", a handsome residence at 11 River Street. He and his wife, the former Margaret Henderson, were married on August 8, 1877. Their son Gordon kept a scrapbook where he pasted clippings about his mother which portray her at three different stages in her life and illustrate how women of her day presented themselves to society. First as a bride, she was beautiful in all her Victorian finery:

> ... attired in white satin à la Princess, trimmed with handsome Honiton lace, a profusion of tulle interspersed with bouquets of orange blossoms and lilies of the valley, and wearing a mantle veil of tulle, wreath and flowers to correspond to the robe. The bridesmaids were costumed in white satin covered with grenadine, decorated with pink moss rosebuds, each wearing a long white tulle veil and a wreath composed of pink rosebuds.

The ceremony was at noon and after it the guests "repaired in carriages to the residence of the bride's father on Gerrard Street" for the "customary dejeuner". The wedding presents, which were "very costly" were on display, "the total value being estimated at about $2,000 and included a diamond set of jewellery, a piano and a marble-top gilt table."

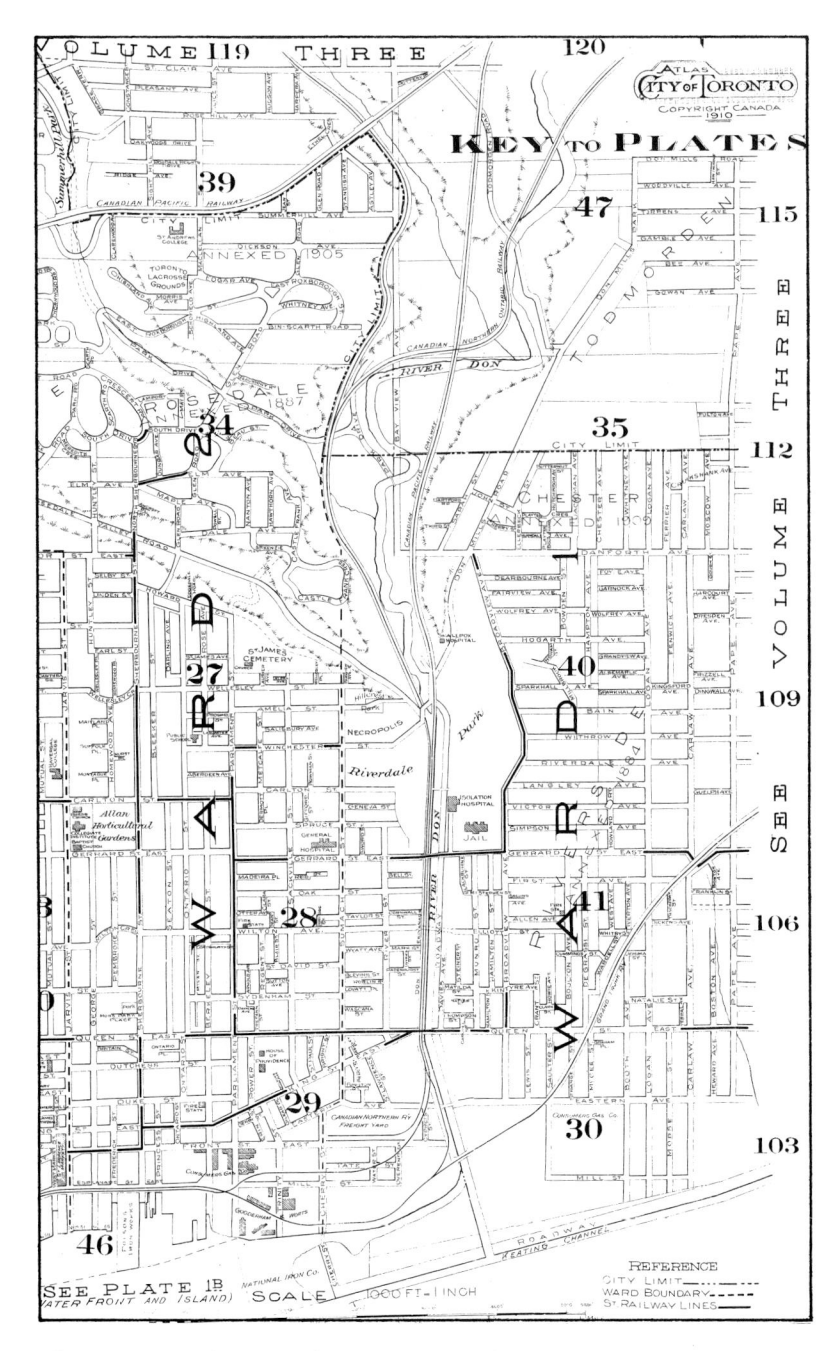

The Don River after it had been straightened.
Atlas of the City of Toronto and Suburbs, 1890, C.E. Goad

River Villa, residence of Alderman Thomas Davies, 11 River Street, built 1880.
Collection of Douglas Davies

Margaret is next seen as a hostess at "Rivervilla" where she received her guests in the library, wearing a matronly gown of grey striped Bedford cord with passementerie trim. It was a grand affair with dancing to Marciano and his orchestra in the drawing room where the floor had been covered with linen sheets. For those who did not dance, card tables had been set up in the dining room and library, while upstairs promenades under shaded lights were "encouraged". The other ladies were most elaborately gowned in brocades, silks, and satins which featured the Empire style, ruchings of lace and loops of satin, velvet sleeves in contrasting colours, bandeaux of otter and feathers set off by diamonds and pearls. Miss Davies, her unmarried sister-in-law, was notable for her diamond tiara and Mrs. Jack King was described as "bright and sparkling as ever as she flitted about like a beautiful butterfly in her gown of white chiffon with a Watteau back and puffed sleeves of green velvet".

Alderman Thomas Davies, 1845-1916.
Collection of George Taylor Gale

In the third clipping, Mrs. Davies is older and sedately gowned in purple satin with a lace yoke and frill for an "At Home" in honour of her daughter-in-law, Mrs. T.A. Davies, who received the guests wearing her wedding gown. This delightful custom of a tea in honour of a new bride gave her the opportunity to wear

Margaret Henderson Davies, 1854-1936.
Collection of George Taylor Gale

her dress once more, and what young woman would not welcome the occasion to appear in "cream duchess satin with drapery of Brussels lace on the corsage and skirt, the train of which was raised at the side with a large cabochon pearl"? The ladies in the reception room where tea was served were gowned in brocade

Robert Davies, 1849-1916.
Collection of George Taylor Gale

with lace and diamonds and Miss Davies of the tiara wore pale blue satin with an overdress of cherry and white brocade. The bride greeted her mother-in-law's guests carrying a sheaf of pink roses and lily of the valley, and the tea room was decorated with baskets of gold and russet chrysanthemums and trailing ferns.

Joseph, the middle brother, was not as well-known as his other brothers and was associated with various family breweries

Margaret Taylor Davies, 1849-1931.
Collection of George Taylor Gale

all his life. In later years, he and his brother-in-law, Thomas B. Taylor, worked together. The real star of the family, however, was Robert, the youngest son, who married George Taylor's daughter Margaret. They first lived at 40 Sumach Street, not far from his Dominion Brewery on Queen Street, but as business improved and their family grew to six sons and three daughters, they moved to William Gooderham's house at 397 Sherbourne Street on the north-east corner of Carlton Street. The Roman

Thorncliffe Farms, owned by Robert Davies.
Collection of Adele Davies Rockwell

Catholic Church of Sacre Coeur was later built on the site. For their summer house, Robert bought "Chester Park" in Todmorden from his wife's aunt, Henrietta Taylor, for $34,000 in 1885. [21] Three years later when his sister Henrietta decided that she had had enough of the country, he bought his brother-in-law T.B. Taylor's valley property (about 600 acres) at the Forks of the Don. He paid $50,000 for this and assumed the mortgages. [22] These sums of money reflect the success of the Dominion Brewery. It could not have been otherwise when Davies was reputed to have been the owner at one time of 144 of Toronto's taverns. [23]

    Probably the farm property was the real turning point in Davies' life. He had always had a passion for horses and Thorncliffe Farms, named after the Taylor house on the property, "Thorn Cliff", became a show-place. Thousands visited it over the years for it had been turned into one of the best equipped stock farms in Canada. Robert was a fine horseman himself and was considered to be "an excellent judge of a trotter, familiar with the blood-lines of the best harness horses and few reinsmen

Dominion Brewery, 412-468 Queen Street East. (Restored).
Century Revenue Properties

ever excelled him". [24] In 1865, when he was only fifteen, he rode a horse called "Nora Crena" for Edward Lepper in the Queen's Plate held at London. Because of this, he had the reputation of being the only owner of race horses in Canada ever to have ridden in the Queen's Plate. He later won this race with a horse called "Floss" which he leased and ran at Kingston in 1871, but he never won with his own horses. It was one of the few prizes that eluded him.

At Thorncliffe Farms he developed one of the largest string of race horses in the country and became one of the leading breeders of thoroughbreds, Clydesdales and standard breds. His racing colours of canary yellow and black were a familiar sight for many years on both the Canadian and American race tracks and when the Connaught Cup was offered for the first time, he decided that it should be on the sideboard in the dining room at "Chester Park". He won it for three successive years with a flying black horse called "Plate Glass", but perhaps his best horse was a steeplechaser called "Thorncliffe" who raced on the difficult course of Old Woodbine at a period when "smashing steeplechase horses was frequent". [25] Robert Davies loved horses and at Thorncliffe he kept the "faithful pensioners, faithful steeds for which he developed a fondness, so much so that he would not sell any one of them for any amount of money offered". [26]

He was president of the Canadian Horse Breeders' Association, a member of the Toronto Hunt Club, an honorary director of the Toronto Exhibition and a vice-president of the Ontario Jockey Club. Locally he was called "King Bob" and was described as

> . . . a masterful man—hence the name—of positive and determined nature and once he decided on his course, he pursued it without flinching. A characteristic instance of his adherence to his determination was the manner of his withdrawal from the office of First Vice-President of the Ontario Jockey Club as a result of a difference with the board over a matter of apparently little importance. On more than one occasion, the late Mr. William Hendrie, the club's president endeavoured to prevail upon him to return to the board urging that the reason for his withdrawal was too trivial for such a step . . .[27]

Molly McLean, whose father was the proprietor of the *Toronto World* and a neighbour in the valley, recalled another incident:

> *One time King Bob, as he was called, had said that he would sell a certain thoroughbred horse that he disliked called Garter King. "Done" said my father, "how much?" Well, said Mr. Davies, you write what you think and I'll write what I think and we'll exchange slips. They both had written $25 as their price. Davies was a better judge of horses than W.F. for later on Garter King got out of control on Jarvis Street, whirling up to a very ornate iron fence which surrounded the Reinhardt residence and temporarily dispensing with the buggy jumped over the lawn amongst the iron deer, dwarfs, etc. which so lavishly decorated the lawn.* [28]

Thorncliffe Farms was Davies's recreation, but business was his first consideration. Described as "a masterful man with a positive and determined way of getting what he wanted", [29] he also had a genius for choosing good employees, according to Dr. Edith Taylor, who knew him. Opinion about him varied but she felt that he was often the victim of an "absurd jealousy". His niece, Mrs. George Gale, was more critical and spoke of his penchant for borrowing money from members of his own family without paying them interest and had doubts about the way he managed her mother's affairs after her father T.B. Taylor died. Robert was an astute businessman, but the most serious accusations about his methods came from the role he played in the affairs of his wife's family. This caused so much acrimony that cousins who had once been friends were forbidden to speak to each other again. The Taylors took him to court and not only did *Taylor v. Davies* set a legal precedent, it significantly influenced the downfall of the Taylor family in East York.

Two seemingly unrelated events set the stage for this: first, in 1900, at the age of fifty-two, Davies sold the Dominion Brewery to an English syndicate and the following year, Taylor Brothers declared bankruptcy. As a major creditor, Robert Davies was free to take advantage of the financial mess of his wife's family. It would have been no secret that the Taylor firm was in trouble, for in the last years of the century the mills had not been

Edna Taylor   Delia Davies

First cousins and once close friends, they never spoke to each other after the bankruptcy.
Author's collection

doing well, the economy was depressed and to cover the losses, the Taylors had been borrowing heavily.

All had gone well for the firm in the 1880s which was a prosperous time and, in retrospect, a golden decade for the Taylors before the disasters of the nineties. Most of the forty-four members of this generation had married and were raising families. Those who lived in Todmorden continued in a style expected of the family regarded as the local gentry and who employed most of the residents of the area. Visitors came from the city and the Taylors travelled back and forth to Toronto to shop and pay their calls on days specified in the *Toronto Blue Book*. Mrs. T.B. Taylor received on the second and fourth Mondays of each month, Mrs. Thomas Taylor was "at home" with her two unmarried daughters, Florence and Ellen, on Jarvis Street, and Mrs. William Taylor received at "Bellehaven". George Taylor, the patriarch of the family, invited everyone to a family reunion "pic-nic" in Routledge's Bush starting at 10 o'clock in

180

Author's collection

the morning, August 5th, 1885. Printed invitations were sent decorated with a picture of "Beechwood" and an inset drawing of his original frame house circled in the corner.[30] When George celebrated his seventy-eighth birthday on October 1st, 1881, his nephew T.B. gave him a handsome gold-topped ebony walking cane engraved to mark the occasion. These were the years marked by the joys and sadnesses, the triumphs and disasters which characterize all large families. The second Mrs. Taylor looked after George at "Beechwood", where his unmarried daughter Emily also lived. She played the piano at the Don Mills Church and when she died at the age of forty-six, the family attributed it to an over-fondness for patent medicines. Carrie, her twin sister, adored diamonds and wore one the size of a large pea in each ear. Her husband, "Dear Arch", was "with the bank" but they were not affluent, and when she and her daughters ran up too many bills shopping at John Catto's on King Street, her brother Will always paid. Their sister Louisa was married to William Tasker, a musician, whose family owned a jewellery store in Toronto and manufactured silver goods. Each year, the Don Mills Church held its two-day Sunday school picnic, one day for the children and one for the adults and the Don Mills

Archibald Henderson, 1856-1898.
Collection of George Taylor Gale

Caroline Taylor Henderson.
Collection of George Taylor Gale

Emily Taylor, 1854-1900.
Caroline Henderson's twin.
Collection of George Taylor Gale

Thomas Defries and William Taylor, photographed on their trip to Florida.
Author's collection

Road was lined with horses and buggies that had come out from the city for the event.

In 1887, William Taylor went to Florida to recover from a bout of pleurisy with a friend, one of the Defries. On the way home, they decided to get off the train and attend the Kentucky Derby. It was a damp day, and the track was slow, and Will decided to put his money on a dappled grey who looked to him like a "mudder", a horse that runs well on wet ground. The odds were enormous and the horse won. But Will's winnings did not go unnoticed and he and Defries were invited to a friendly game of poker by the proverbial Kentucky colonels. Will soon realized what they had in mind and after loosing a few hands, he began to play in earnest and won all their money. It was a story he told many times with great delight.

These were the successful years and led to the establishment of the brick mill in the Don Valley. To finance this large operation, John F. Taylor arranged for two large loans from his father. The first amounted to $50,000, which George borrowed from the estate of his deceased brother-in-law James Worts. [31] John F. Taylor arranged a second loan of $120,000 from his father in 1892 with a mortgage on seven parcels of land representing the collateral. [32] This transaction occurred about the same time that George Taylor suffered the stroke that led to his death eighteen months later. This misfortune may have provided the incentive to put his affairs in order. He signed his will in December 1892 and, to ensure that his five daughters received their share of the estate, John F. and his two brothers signed a declaration of trust by which they agreed that the $120,000 was held in trust by them for their sisters and that, in the event of their father's death, interest payments would be made to the sisters. [33] George also transferred his interest in the Worts mortgage to his three sons so that it was no longer part of his estate, and as a further move, his three sons agreed to pay an annuity to their step-mother after their father's death. [34]

George Taylor died on Thursday, the 17th of May, 1894 and his funeral was the occasion for the family to publically proclaim its pioneer origins and achievements. In the obituary in the newspaper, it was said that George was "one of the most widely known men in York Township" and was called a "pioneer of the paper industry in Canada". [35] An Anglican and a Methodist minister were asked to conduct the service which took place at "Beechwood" at three o'clock the following Saturday. The Reverend Arthur Sanson from Little Trinity, who was by then very old, had been a friend of the family since the 1840s when he had ridden out to the Don Valley on horseback from St. John's, York Mills Anglican Church to conduct the service at John

Taylor's house at the Forks of the Don. William B. Booth, who gave the eulogy, later served as the minister at the Don Mills Methodist Church that the Taylors had given to the community. His address was entitled "The Righteous Dead" and it was typical of Victorian sentiment and overstatement, but also somehow appropriate:

> *Thou shalt be missed, because thy seat will be empty. How true of the departed! How true in the Don Mills Church, where he was a most faithful attendant! True, not only because there is a vacant seat, but because there is the absence of a strong and striking personality that brought into the service a reverence, and an inspiration felt alike by preacher and people. He was quiet and undemonstrative in his manner of worship, but his faith was deep-seated, abiding in the Eternal and in his Son, Jesus Christ, while his hope penetrated beyond the clouds and his love encompassed all. But his influence was not confined to the Church. It was extended throughout the community. His presence was felt wherever he went. The commanding force of his character made him a king among men. His life was a perpetual sermon on the subjects of industry, honesty, Sabbath-keeping, fidelity to a plain pure Protestant faith, loyalty to our great Empire, liberality to the needy, kindness to the sick and sorrowing, and such things as build up a noble character and develop true manhood . . .* [36]

The large assembly gathered on the lawn of the house and moved off in the pouring rain for the funeral procession to the family cemetery nearby. The pall-bearers were George's former business associates: George A. Cox, one of the richest men in Canada; W.H. Beatty, who had married George's niece Charlotte Worts; and Robert Kilgour, another director of the Bank of Commerce; W.B. Hamilton and Major A.M. Crosby, who were fellow directors from the London and Ontario Investment Company and James Austin, an old friend, whose wife was called Aunt Austin by George's children. The Mayor of Toronto regretted that he was unable to attend because he was ill. This was the last great gathering of the Taylor family which displayed it in all its wealth and importance.

Notes

1. *Mail and Empire,* "Thomas Davies", September 20, 1916; *Toronto Star,* "300 Gooderham Descendants to Meet . . .", n.d. (family collection).
2. R.D. Defries, "The Robert Defries Family" (author's collection, unpublished, 1969)
3. *Toronto Directory,* 1872-1873, p. 209.
4. *Ibid.,* opposite p. 209.
5. Adele Davies Rockwell, conversation with the author.
6. *The Commemorative Biographical Record* (Toronto: J.H. Beers Co., 1907), p. 105.
7. *Toronto World,* March 23, 1916, "Bob Davies One of Toronto's Wealthiest".
8. Adele Davies Rockwell, conversation with the author.
9. *The Commemorative Biographical Record,* p. 105; *History of the County of York* (Toronto: C. Blackett Robinson, 1885), 2 vols. v. II, p. 379.
10. *Ibid.,* p. 379.
11. *Acorn,* Vols. 1-3, 1976-78, Summer 1977, p. 5.
12. R.D. Defries, p. 4.
13. *Ibid.,* p. 9.
14. J. Temperlake, *Illustrated Toronto Past and Present* (Toronto: Peter A. Gross, 1877), pp. 267-269.
15. *Ibid.,* p. 270.
16. *Ibid.*
17. *Ibid.*
18. *Globe,* September 20, 1919, "Thomas Davies Dead".
19. *Ibid.*
20. *Evening Telegram,* September 8, 1913, "Don Swept Bridges to Lake".
21. (TMA), Inventory of Historical Houses in East York, p. 42.
22. R.O. #30459, November 3, 1888.
23. Edwin C. Guillet, *Pioneer Inns and Taverns* (Toronto: author, 1954), p. 101.
24. *The Globe,* 23 March, 1916, "King Bob is Dead".

25. *Ibid.*
26. *Ibid.*
27. *Ibid.*
28. (TMA), Letters to Charles Sauriol.
29. *The Globe,* 23 March, 1916, "King Bob is Dead".
30. In possession of the author.
31. R.O. #38742, #38743, May 27, 1891.
32. R.O. #41627, December 21, 1892.
33. R.O. #41628, December 22, 1892.
34. Will of George Taylor, probate, January 28, 1895.
35. Mrs. George Taylor, scrapbook, undated, in the possession of the author.
36. *Ibid.*

Louise Taylor Tasker, 1907.
Author's collection

VIII

TAYLOR vs DAVIES

After George's death, Taylor Brothers went downhill and the letters and papers of Louisa Tasker, one of George's daughters, give some indication of what happened. In a letter written to her on December 21, 1896, Mr. Worrell, K.C., the family lawyer from the firm of Crombie, Worrell and Gwynne, stated that "Mr. Taylor tells me everything is in good shape from a business point of view and that it is expected that a dividend will soon be paid". This, it will be remembered, would have been her share of the interest on the loan of $120,000 to Taylor Brothers which she and her sisters inherited from their father. However, a depression began at this time in all the building trades, particularly for the owners of quarries like the Taylors, and from this date until well after 1900 there was a decline in construction, employment, wages and, consequently, in the demand for bricks. In 1898, Mr. Worrell wrote to Mrs. Tasker that he was "acting on what I understand is your desire... I have not pressed for payment" and that he believed that "Mr. Taylor expects to be able to settle the matter..."[11]; but another undated letter states that Messrs. Taylor Brothers "expect to be able to effect a sale of a portion of their property in the near future..."

Through no fault of the firm, building in Toronto was declining and with it the demand for the products of the Don Valley Pressed Brick Works. Worse was to follow; John F. Taylor, the senior partner and business manager, was forced to retire from active business because of ill-health and died on September 11, 1901 at the age of fifty-four. On November 14, 1900 a fire destroyed the Lower Mill completely and the fact that the owners had not been able to insure their property against loss is an indication of how serious the state of the firm's affairs had become.[2] Furthermore, although it cannot be verified,

In the Matter of
William Thomas Taylor
George Arthur Taylor and
John Frederick Taylor
trading under the firm name of
Taylor Brothers
— and —
William Thomas Taylor
and George Arthur Taylor
Individually.

Statement
of Affairs
14th June 1901.

Collection of Ronald R. Tasker

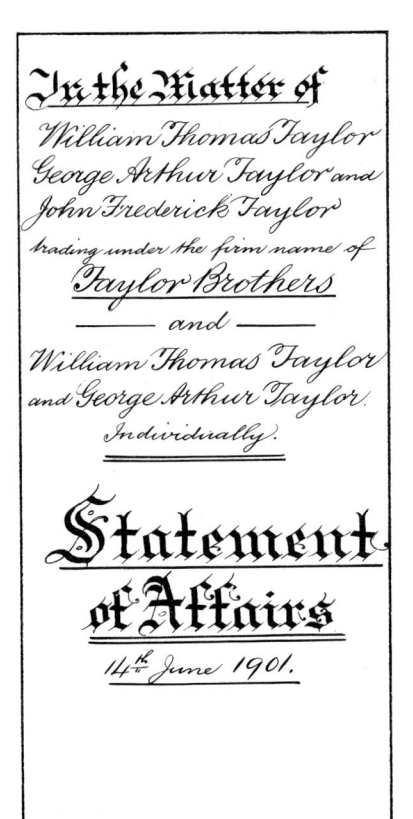

E.R.C. Clarkson.
The Story of the Firm, 1864-1964;
Clarkson Gordon & Co.

George Carruthers, who interviewed members of the family years later for his book, *Paper in the Making,* asserts "that owing to the defection of one of their employees, the firm went bankrupt". [3] No one has been able to discover who this employee was or how much money was involved. However, for a combination of reasons, the Taylor firm declared bankruptcy on June 14, 1901. [4]

There has always been a stigma attached to bankruptcy, which seems to signify failure and mismanagement and carries with it a degree of social ostracism, shame and embarrassment.

John F. Taylor escaped all of this by dying, and either he was able to salvage his own fortune in time or the money came from his wife's family, the Pattersons, for his widow and daughter were unaffected by the demise of Taylor Brothers. It was debatable if George Arthur, the second partner in the firm, ever understood what had happened, but William, the youngest brother, was left in charge and for this he was not prepared. He had always attended to the practical aspects of the firm and had left the business decisions to his older brother. It was now his duty to cope with the proceedings and legalities. It was all the more tragic for him because in the events which followed he was the victim of his own inexperience.

The auditors appointed as trustee the well-known and respected E.R.C. Clarkson who had a "fine reputation in the business community" and was said to "be able to wind up a business quickly and realize cash for creditors". [5] The Clarkson firm is still in business in Toronto; the Clarkson in question, who had followed his father Thomas' footsteps, had received his appointment as Official Assignee in 1881, become a chartered accountant in 1883 and was one of the members of the first council of the Institute of Chartered Accountants and Adjustors in Canada. [6] His firm of Clarkson and Cross looked after accountancy, trustee and bankruptcy work. (It must be a coincidence, but indicative of the smallness of Toronto, that Clarkson's mother had been Sarah Helliwell, who was related to the Helliwells of the Don Valley.)

As trustee, Clarkson's first duty was to publish an announcement of the Taylor firm's insolvency in the *Ontario Gazette* and the newspapers, after which he registered the assignment and called a meeting of the creditors. This was held at two o'clock on the afternoon of July 5th at his office in the Ontario Bank Chambers on Scott Street where he presented a statement of affairs. At this meeting, as specified in the banktruptcy legislation, six inspectors of the estate were appointed from among the creditors present and were given "power in conjunction with the Assignee to realize upon the assets to the best advantage" and who were "to superintend and direct the proceedings of the Assignee in the management and winding up of the estate". [7] According to the minutes of the meeting, these inspectors were two brothers-in-law of the Taylors, David Smith and Robert

> ONTARIO BANK CHAMBERS,
> SCOTT STREET,
>
> TORONTO, July 5th, 1901.
>
> MINUTES OF MEETING of Creditors of TAYLOR BROS. held at the office of E. R. C. Clarkson, Assignee, this day at two o'clock p.m.
>
> There were present:—
>
> MR. J. A. WORRELL, K.C.
> MR. ROBT. DAVIES.
> MR. E. J. W. OWENS.
> THE MANAGER OF THE QUEBEC BANK.
> MR. DAVID SMITH
> MR. FRANK DENTON, K.C.
> MR. NOEL MARSHALL.
> MR. HUSON MURRAY, K.C.
> MR. MARSH.
> MR. J. T. ROLPH,
> and a number of others.
>
> The Assignee presented and read Statement of Affairs.
>
> On motion of Mr. J. A. Worrell, K.C., it was resolved, that Messrs. E. J. W. Owens, David Smith, Robert Davies, Frank Denton, K.C., J. A. Worrell, K.C. and Carrington Smith be appointed Inspectors of the Estate, with power in conjunction with the Assignee to realize upon the assets to the best advantage.
>
> The meeting adjourned *sine die.*
>
> A meeting of the Inspectors was held immediately afterwards when it was decided as follows:
>
> That the Assignee should ask Mr. Burls for a tender for the purchase of the Market St. stock and the book debts. That the Paper Mill be continued running until the raw material is made up, and that offers be asked from the trade for the purchase of the paper. That Mr. Burls' tender should include the printing plant, store and office furniture. That Mr. Bowman be retained to sell the bricks at list prices as near as may be, and that when the stock brick is sold the balance be disposed of by public auction. That the real estate be offered for sale by public auction, the Assignee to procure valuations of the same, excepting the brick-yard and the property covered by the mortgage held by Mr. Worrell as Trustee. The Conditions of Sale of the last two parcels to provide that the purchaser buys the property subject to encumbrances, and to lease of the brick-yard to Mr. Davies for sufficient time to enable him to make all bricks contracted for by him up to the day of sale.
>
> Terms of sale as to the other properties, where mortgaged—the amount of the above mortgage to be paid in cash, where not mortgaged, forty per cent. cash, balance on time at five per cent.
>
> Mr. Davies took the list of chattels on the farms and said he would report as to their value.
>
> The Assignee was instructed to discount a note at the Quebec Bank and pay the wages of the employees.
>
> Mr. Owens was requested to write to Mr. Dun in charge of the Leys' farm, to come to town and arrange as to what is to be done with the property.

Collection of Ronald R. Tasker

Davies, E.J. Owens, Frank Denton, the Taylors' lawyer J.A. Worrell representing the five sisters, and Carrington Smith. [8] They met immediately after the creditors meeting and made their decisions.

First of all, it was decided to dispose of the stock, printing plant, store and office furniture at the Market Street office. They agreed to keep the paper mill running until the stock of raw material was used and then to offer the paper to the trade. All the bricks on hand at the Don Valley Pressed Brick Works were to be sold at list prices and then the balance of the mill was to be sold at public auction. This decision to have an auction was to have great importance in later events. In addition, the Taylors'

Robert Davies.
Collection of George Taylor Gale

real estate was to be auctioned except the brick yard, which was to be leased to Robert Davies "for sufficient time to enable him to make all bricks contracted for by him up to the day of the sale", and the property covered by Mr. Worrell as trustee for the Worts estate. [9] The terms of the sale of the other properties, where mortgaged, was the amount of the mortgage and on the unmortgaged land it was to be 40%. A note at the Quebec Bank was to be discounted, the employees paid their wages and in addition, Robert Davies agreed to list the chattels on the farm and report on their value. The Taylors owned two farms in Pickering, one of them the Elliott farm (Lot 11, Concession IV) which had belonged to their Aunt Edith. In addition, they owned land in Haliburton and Wentworth County, and had lots on Pape Avenue, Langley, Steiner and Gerrard Streets as well as houses in Todmorden and on Victor Avenue.

The Statement of Affairs prepared by Clarkson showed that their debts amounted to $213,156, their assets to $78,000 and that their "nominal deficiency" was consequently $135,130. [10] The list of their creditors was extensive and included the Quebec Bank, the Trust and Loan Company, the Freehold Loan Company, the Toronto Mortgage Company and various estates. The largest creditors were the five sisters who had lent their brothers the $120,000 under the trust which was secured by a first mortgage on the homestead, on a further 350 acres and on the Middle Paper Mill and by a second mortgage on lots on the Don Mills Road, Leslie Street and Woodville Avenue. The other major creditor was the Taylors' brother-in-law, Robert Davies, who had lent the firm $100,000, secured by the brickyard plant and 140 acres of land in the Don Valley. It was this second large loan from Davies that proved so crucial in future events.

At the time of the first meeting, the creditors agreed that Mr. Clarkson would be responsible for preparing accounts and statements informing the creditors of how the estate was being managed. He was assisted in this by the inspectors, who were required to verify the bank balance, examine the trustee's accounts and approve his final statement of receipts and disbursements. Clarkson was also required to pay "as large a dividend as can be paid with safety" within a year and this was to be repeated every six months until the estate was wound up. [11] This accorded with usual practice and the Taylors accepted the results. [12] A small dividend was realized and the ordinary creditors were paid, but the two Taylor brothers, George and William, got nothing.

What was not revealed at the first meeting of creditors, however, was that earlier, on June 25, 1901, Clarkson and Robert Davies had held a private meeting concerning the brickyard. Clarkson appears to have assumed from the outset that the brick plant and lands upon which it stood could not be sold for an amount sufficient to pay the Davies mortgage and still leave anything for the creditors, let alone the Taylors. Since the amount due under the Davies mortgage exceeded the value of the property, he agreed to rent the brick works to Davies for one month at a rental of $25. Davies took possession and carried on the business. He spent considerable sums on improvements and acted as if he was the outright owner, rather than temporary occupant under a lease. It is not certain whether or not the meeting of the creditors was informed that Davies was already in possession of the brickyard under the Clarkson lease. No auction of the property ever took place and Clarkson had the brickyard appraised by two surveyors, who put a value of $45,000 on the lands, buildings and machinery. This in itself seems suspect, because the appraisal was somewhat superficial and the surveyors in question had no special knowledge of the brickmaking business.

Further discussions and negotiations took place between Clarkson and Davies and, although there is no firm evidence of this, a deed for the brickyard properties was prepared for Davies by his solicitors and sent to Clarkson for execution in February 1902. The inspectors met again on April 22, 1902 and accepted the $45,000 valuation. They also agreed that the brickyard property should be conveyed to Davies at that price and that he should rank as an ordinary creditor for the balance of his claim under the mortgage. This was contrary to his role as an inspector, which the law clearly defined: "an inspector shall not directly or indirectly purchase any part of the stock-in-trade, debts or other assets of the assignor... inspectors must not in any way make a profit at the expense of the estate". [13] Mr. J.A. Worrell, acting for the Taylor sisters, doubted the propriety of this transaction since Davies, as an inspector, was not entitled to profit in any way. He wrote to Clarkson advising him that it should be confirmed by the creditors. A meeting was called, but it was very sparsely attended and a resolution approving the transaction passed with little or no dissent. The notice of this meeting was also insufficient and did not give the creditors any real information as to the transaction to be sanctioned.

It was unfortunate that John F. Taylor, the businessman of the family, was too ill to attend the meeting, for he alone would have been able to question the proceedings of Clarkson and the inspectors. As a result of this meeting, a deed from Clarkson to Davies was duly executed and delivered to Davies in September 1902. Davies thus became owner of the most valuable part of the Taylor property for $45,000 without any real attempt being made to ascertain its proper value or to find an alternate buyer.

The remaining assets of the insolvent estate were realized in due course, but produced only enough to provide a small dividend for the ordinary creditors and left nothing for the Taylor brothers. They seem to have accepted the result, raising no objections when the brickworks were turned over to Robert Davies.

Within a year, the name of the Don Valley Pressed Brick Works was changed to the Don Valley Brick Works and was being advertised under the heading of "Bricks, Bricks, Bricks...", perhaps an unconscious expression of Davies' exuberance over the coup he had achieved. [14] Business at the brick works prospered, aided in part by the improved economy, until, by the time of Davies' death in 1916, it was said to be "the world's largest brick plant". [15] Davies had been a shrewd businessman; in the same way that he had managed his brewery, he devoted his energy to this new endeavour and became such an expert that at one time he was president of the Canadian Clay Products Association. [16]

On the other hand, John F. Taylor's business ability could not compare to his brother-in-law's. He had been responsible for the accumulation of debts that led to his company's bankruptcy. He himself was forced to sell his house, "Fernwood Place", in September 1901 and it was bought by Robert L. Patterson for $8,000. [17] He and his wife Sasha lived in the house until 1930 when it was sold to the present owners, the Ina Grafton Gage Home of the United Church of Canada, for $45,000. [18] A certain amount of glamour was attached to Sasha Patterson because of her name. Some said that she was a Russian countess, but Walter Taylor, who knew her, said that she was the daughter of a former United States ambassador to Russia.

After John F. Taylor died, his wife and daughter Kate spent the rest of their lives at 98 Spadina Road; their fortune remained considerable. Kate never married and when she came to the family gatherings in the 1940s, she was always driven by a uniformed chauffeur in a limousine. On her death, she left a

George Arthur Taylor.
Author's collection

large part of her estate to the Banting Institute for cancer research and legacies to three cousins, the daughters of her aunt Caroline Henderson, who lived at "Beechwood". [19] She had inherited the house from her father George Taylor, and when she died in about 1915 she left it to her daughters. [20] They sold it in 1945 after it had been in the family for over a hundred years and it remains the oldest house in the Borough of East York. [21]

9 Hassard Avenue. Early records for this house list its address as 9 Hawthorne Row. Hawthorne was the maiden name of George Taylor's mother and on this street he built houses which he let to the more senior and important workers in the Taylor mills. This particular home was built there around 1872. In 1904, with the dissolution of part of the Taylor Estate (after the death of Emily Taylor), the house was sold to the Bray Family. Todmorden Mills Archives

11 and 13 Hassard Avenue. Like 9 Hassard, these were homes built by George Taylor for his more important workmen. This building is somewhat earlier than 9 Hassard, being built about 1854. At various times these homes were lived in by two of the Taylor's best known employees. George Rice and his family lived there between 1890 and 1904. Mr. Rice was notable for his introduction of piece-work to the Don Valley Pressed Brick Works. This process was credited at the time with having saved the business from bankruptcy and making it the profitable firm it remains today. After 1904 the Samuel Vernon family lived in one of these units. Mr. Vernon was responsible for the emigration of more than 200 English families to East York to work at the brick factory.
Todmorden Mills Archives

Fortunately, William Taylor's house was in his wife's name and did not have to be sold. William and a new partner, Charles Thomson, leased the Middle Mill from Robert Davies who had a security claim on it. [22] The Thomsons owned the Napanee Paper Company at New Berg, near Kingston, and it may have been a matter of expanding the business that brought Mr. Thomson to Toronto. One of his employees, Clayton Fletcher Ash, had started working in the Thomson Mill when he was fourteen and in 1889 moved to Toronto and was employed by the Taylors. He was recommended by Mr. White, who also knew the Thomsons, and when Mr. White retired, Ash succeeded him as manager of the Lower Mill. The Taylors provided houses for a number of their employees and the Ash family lived on Hawthorne Row near O'Connor Drive and Pape Avenue at the eastern extremity of land owned by Louise Tasker, one of George Taylor's five daughters. It is difficult to determine just how many houses the Taylors built for their workmen, but the two semi-detached houses at 11 and 13 Hassard Avenue in East York have been identified as their constructions. [23] The Statement of Affairs prepared at the time of the bankruptcy noted five cottages on the family homestead, "Beechwood", and lots on Woodville, Torrens, Gamble and Bee Avenues which may also have housed mill workers. These houses were rented and the income from the rents distributed among members of the family. The Ashes later moved to a house in Chester Village and when Clayton Ash became the manager of the Lower Mill in 1899, the family moved again to John Eastwood's stone house at the foot of the Pottery Road hill near the mill. William Taylor and his bride had lived there before they built "Bellehaven" at the top of the hill. Eastwood had built the house in 1832, but unfortunately this charming stone building (pictured in Robertson's *Landmarks of Toronto*) [24] burned down. Edna Ash, Clayton's daughter, remembers it well and said that it contained a ballroom on the ground floor. One likes to think that it was here that those early settlers in the valley, the Helliwells, Skinners, and Eastwoods, danced their jigs and reels.

William soon sold out his interest to Charles Thomson and in 1907 Robert Davies bought the mill outright. [25] With the help of Clayton Ash, Davies made plans to renovate the operations. Together they went to Three Rivers to look at other paper mills

Collection of Adele Davies Rockwell

and Ash was sent several times to Worcester, Massachusetts where the 84-inch Harper Fourdrinier machine was overhauled at Rice, Barton and Fales. In July, 1909 the mill was restarted as the Don Valley Paper Company Limited and was described in the *Pulp and Paper Magazine of Canada* as a model mill of its day: "refurbished on a lavish but business-like scale... with up to date machinery and equipment of a class to turn out the very best product in an economical manner". [26] There were seven buildings occupying a total length of about 350 feet, constructed of brick and cement and of an average length of 40 to 60 feet. All the machinery was on a bed-plate set in concrete to a depth of eight feet and the mill was heated by steam and lit by electricity produced on the premises. It had extensive fire protection equipment and a room had been provided for a factory to make paper bags with 30 to 40 machines, and adjoining it was a lunch room for the women who worked there. To facilitate shipments of paper and to bring in supplies of pulp and coal, a railway siding ran right into the buildings. It was considered exemplary for the paper industry since every effort was made to save labour. Pulp was specially imported from Sweden and this was used to make Kraft papers and fine manilla. [27]

The Ash family moved to 360 Don Mills Road (now Broadview Avenue) where they lived until Mr. Ash retired in 1910. Next door at 388 Don Mills Road lived the Diefenbacker (later

| Phone North 1829 |
| Phone North 244 |

Toronto, _____ *191*___

SUN BRICK CO., LIMITED
═══BRICK MANUFACTURERS═══
WORKS: Don Valley, TORONTO

Sun Brick Co., Limited, 1911.
Author's collection

Diefenbaker) family who were there for about a year in 1906 before they moved to western Canada. Mr. Diefenbacker was the principal of the Plains Road school east of Pape Avenue, which his two sons Elmer and John attended. He played the piano and gave music lessons to Jessie Taylor, one of John H. Taylor's daughters. The music lessons made little impression, but in later years she was proud to relate that she had taken young John, the future Prime Minister of Canada, to school. [28]

While his brother-in-law Robert Davies was pouring money into the brick and paper mills, William Taylor decided to make one more effort to do what he knew best. He persuaded his friend Henry Pellat (he was not knighted until some years later) to lend him money to start another brick mill. Together with William Booth, a lumberman, he began work on the Sun Brick

Collection of Ronald R. Tasker

Company about 1908 on parts of Lot 15, Concession II FB and Lot 11, Concession III FB. [29] The company was not incorporated until 1911 and William was not listed as a partner, no doubt because of the damage to his business reputation at the time of the bankruptcy. It was registered instead in the name of his wife and their daughter Edna and the names of William Booth, G.W. Booth, T.W. Booth and W.A. Werrett, a solicitor. [30] The company lasted only a year until new owners took over, but continued in operation until the 1930s. [31]

Feelings between the Davies and the Taylors in Todmorden during those years were strained, to put it mildly. From "Bellehaven" at the top of Pottery Road, William could see the smoke stacks of the Don Valley Brick Mills puffing away in the valley below, making money for his brother-in-law, and farther up the valley the paper mill was in full production under Davies's capable management. Thorncliffe Farms at the forks of the Don were further evidence of Davies's prosperity. He was also apparently back in the brewing business, managing the Copland Brewery which had been his brother-in-law T.B. Taylor's before his death. After Davies died, two of his sons, Robert and George, inherited an interest in it. [32]

The Taylors felt that he had taken advantage of them, but there was no way of proving it, so they thought, until 1914. In May of that year, it became known that Robert Davies had received $238,583 as payment for 11.58 acres of land which had been expropriated by the Canadian Northern Railway from the brickyards. William went to his lawyers who advised him that there was cause for a law suit. Thus, thirteen years after the bankruptcy, in July 1914, according to legal terminology, Isabella Taylor brought action on her own behalf and behalf of all other persons entitled under the trusts of the assignment for the benefit of creditors alleging that the property conveyed to Davies had a much greater value than the amount owing under the mortgage, that Davies being the inspector at the time was disqualified from purchasing, and that the conveyance was a breach of trust and should be set aside. [33]

Davies himself had had a stroke in 1913 and died in March 1916 before the trial took place and never knew the outcome. It was a complete vindication of the Taylors. The brickyard deal was declared invalid and the newspapers reported "Davies Claim Void, Mrs. Taylor Wins". [34] Mr. Justice Lennox wrote in his long judgement that he dismissed the transfer of the brickyard property from Clarkson, who was representing Taylor Brothers, to the late Robert Davies because there had not been "full and honest disclosure" and that the sale had not been duly advertised. [35] This was a damaging statement to Clarkson's and Davies's integrity. Lennox found that the property was worth far more than the value put on it for conveyance, that Davies as inspector was under an obligation to keep a watch on the assignee, Clarkson, and to see that the assets were realized to the best advantage and was disabled from becoming the purchaser. His Lordship's findings regarding the two men were caustic. He wrote:

The assignee appears to have proceeded very much upon the basis of a worn-out industry. He says so, in effect, and proceeds to value the land as "grazing land". Of the quantity

> or value of brick material as it lay there he took no account, made no inquiry, and knew nothing. I think this material was worth from 30 to 35 cents per cubic yard. This item alone on ordinary output, and on the Davies output, nearly 10,000,000 for the first year of which an account could be obtained runs into a lot of money. I cannot believe that Mr. Davies continued to make outlays and work this property for a year without knowing the character of the business, the approximate saleable value of the property and business, and that he was obtaining it all at a sum far below its saleable value in the open market. [36]

He further held that if there had been proper advertisement of the sale, it would have realised far more than $45,000, the amount of the Davies mortgage, and enough to pay the other creditors entitled to rank on the estate in full. Although the Limitations Act barred actions for the recovery of land after a lapse of ten years, Lennox found that it did not apply. Davies was directed to account for the monies received from the railway company and for the profits which he had made from the business carried on by him since he had taken possession of the lands and plant in 1901.

E.R.C. Clarkson, as trustee for the Taylors, was further chastised by His Lordship:

> I cannot see that this trustee ever really discharged himself from his duties as a trustee. He obtained his position from the creditors; he never professed or attempted to surrender his trust to them or to contract with them for the discharge or the right to become a purchaser. He made no application to the court. He allowed the creditors to separate and when they separated on June 18th, the whole transaction was virtually disposed of. [37]

The Limitations Act was grounds for appeal and this was heard in the Appellate Division of the Supreme Court of Ontario in October 1917. [38] Judgement was given allowing the appeal and dismissing the action, both with costs. Mrs. Taylor thereupon appealed to the Judicial Committee of the Privy Council in England and a third trial took place. [39] Mrs. Taylor's appeal was

William T. Taylor.
Author's collection

dismissed, it being held that the Limitations Act afforded a proper defence to the action, but it is clear from the remarks made by Viscount Cave in giving the Judgement of the Privy Council that had action been brought within the ten-year period the plaintiff would have succeeded. [40]

Five years of litigation had ended in nothing but expense and disappointment for the Taylors and it would have provided little consolation for them to know that *Taylor v. Davies* established an important legal precedent which is still cited as the most important case of its type in the Ontario Courts. Perhaps if John F. Taylor had lived it might have been a different story.

While William and Isabella were obliged to sell "Bellehaven" to pay for legal costs, they were able to make a fortunate agreement with the purchaser. It was bought by James Fransceschini, the president of the Dufferin Construction Company, who wanted a place to dump fill from the excavation for Eaton's College Street store, and as part of the sale he allowed the Taylors to live in the house, rent free, for as long as they lived. The fill was dumped on the edge of the hill at the western edge of the front garden and was hidden from view by a hedge of flowering shrubs. Little did Mr. Fransceschini realize that William would live to be eighty-seven and Isabella would not die until 1951, when she was ninety-four.

New names and new faces came into the community that was still referred to as Todmorden by the long-time residents. After Robert Davies's death, his estate took over his various enterprises and carried on the paper mill until 1928, when it was purchased by Norman E. Wainwright. [41] His company operated it until June 1939, when it was sold to Howard Smith Paper Mills Limited. Howard Smith began operating it as a subsidiary of the Alliance Paper Mills and his grandson, G. Howard Smith, has been the manager since 1956. [42] Some parts of the building, including the tall chimney, remain as a reminder of the original Taylor operations although it was damaged in a fire in 1922 and subsequently renovated. In 1961, Domtar Limited purchased the mill and today it has a unique position in the history of Canada's paper industry. However, its future is in some doubt since, as Mr. Smith has said, "the day of the small specialty mill is coming to an end". [43]

The brick mill was also sold by the Davies estate in 1928 and was owned by Strathgowan Investments and operated under the name of the Toronto Brick Company until 1984. Little remained of the original brickyards except for one decaying brick chimney, one of four that once dominated the property. Each chimney possessed one word of the name Don Valley Brick Works, but few of the original buildings survived. [44]

Robert Davies's sons inherited Thorncliffe Farms and were partners in the Thorncliffe Stock Farms operation, where they bred and raced thoroughbreds in their father's tradition. They won the King's Plate in 1922 and 1929, something their father was never able to do. [45] Some of the Thorncliffe property was sold to financial interests from Baltimore who formed the Thorncliffe Park Racing and Breeding Association Limited and

Wilfred Davies, one of Robert Davies' sons on "Fountain Fey," schooling at Chester Park on Broadview Avenue.
Collection of Adele Davies Rockwell

operated a race track from 1920 until 1952. [46] Then, "Toronto interests bought the track and promptly sold it to Thorncliffe Park Limited which in turn was attached to Leaside in 1954. By this time, Leaside was completely developed and these 380 acres gave the town much needed room for expansion." [47] "Thorn Cliff", the first Taylor house, became more and more derelict and was finally destroyed.

Four Oaks Gate, a subdivision to the north of O'Connor Drive and Don Mills Road, was also named after a Taylor house. This property was owned by John H. Taylor who, in 1929, was farming about 300 acres of the land he had inherited from his father John. He and his cousin William had two characteristics in common: they were both tall, spare men, who as they grew older looked more and more alike, and neither was a good businessman. Most of the property was planted in rye which

After the Don Valley property was sold, another Thorncliffe Farm was established at Thornhill, shown here. Pictured are Wilfred Davies and his trainer Fred Shelke.
Collection of Adele Davies Rockwell

provided so little income that during the Depression John H. Taylor had difficulty paying his taxes. The eleven acres close to the house, "Four Oaks Gate", were planted in corn and tomatoes and provided some revenue. The greengrocers on the Danforth came and picked it for their stores. When he died in 1949, taxes were still a problem, but his son John, a much better businessman, persuaded the Township that it was more profitable to subdivide the land. The valley property, which is now part of the Don Valley Parkway, was sold in order to pay $6,000 in taxes and the rest was divided into lots. Dr. Edith Taylor, one of John H.'s daughters, said that the family was grateful to her brother who managed to do "such a remarkable job out of what had been a ghastly mess".

Taylor Cemetery, East York.
Author's collection

When William Taylor died in 1944, he and Isabella had been married for almost sixty years. He was the last of his generation to be part of the Taylor dynasty in East York and it seems fitting that their story should end with him. The family gathered at "Bellehaven" where black crepe hung on the double front doors in the Victorian tradition, and his coffin lay in state in the north parlour by the grand piano. He himself had chosen the lovely cream, rose and blue oriental rug for this room, the tiles around the marble fireplace and the stained glass panels depicting Greek goddesses in the north window. On the walls were portraits of his father George and his mother Caroline, who had died when he was twelve years old. The funeral service was conducted by the minister from Don Mills United Church, the church his father and uncles had given in 1860 to the Primitive Methodist Connexion, and when the funeral procession moved slowly out of the driveway, Isabella and her daughters and granddaughters sadly watched it leave the house from a tower window upstairs. In those days it was not the custom for women of the family to attend the burial service. William was buried in the family cemetery to the west of the church, and it is ironic that this cemetery is all that remains to the family of the vast holdings they once possessed in the Don Valley.

Notes

1. Dr. R.R. Tasker, in family papers in possession of the author.
2. George Carruthers, *Paper in the Making* (New Jersey: Garden City Press, 1947), p. 317.
3. *Ibid.*
4. *Ontario Law Reports,* 1917, p. 205.
5. J.A. Little, *The Story of the Firm, 1864 - 1964* (Toronto: University of Toronto Press, 1964), p. 18.
6. *Ibid.,* p. 15.
7. Assignments and Preferences Act, *Revised Statutes of Ontario,* Chap. 34, Section 31, p. 247.
8. Dr. R.R. Tasker, Minutes of Meeting of Creditors, family papers.
9. *Ibid.*
10. *Ibid.*
11. Assignments and Preferences Act.
12. Summary of the official law reports of Taylor v. Davies, 1917; O.L.R., p. 205; in the Appelate Division of the Supreme Court of Ontario; 41, O.L.R. and in the Privy Council, 1919, A.C. 636 was prepared by Donald Guthrie, Q.C. and are included as such in the text of the narrative.
13. R.S. Cassels, Ontario Assignments and Preferences Act, 1914, pp. 116-117.
14. *Toronto Directory,* 1902.
15. *The Globe,* March 23, 1916, "Robert Davies Dead".
16. *Ibid.*
17. (TMA), Inventory of Historical Buildings in East York, p. 74.
18. *Ibid.*
19. "Leaves $500,000 to Banting Lab in Cancer Fight", obituary, n.d.; Family Scrapbook, in the possession of the author.

20. R.O. #106474.
21. R.O. #50695, 1945.
22. Ian Howes, "Paper Making in the Don Valley", unpublished, 1981.
23. Inventory of Historical Buildings in East York, p. 63.
24. J.R. Robertson, *Landmarks of Toronto* (Toronto: Toronto Evening Telegram, 1898) 6 vols., v. I, p. 428.
25. George Carruthers, p. 319.
26. "Don Valley Paper Mills" in *Pulp and Paper Magazine*, 1901, p. 238.
27. *Ibid.*
28. Conversation with Dr. Edith Taylor.
29. R.O. #6422, January 20, 1926.
30. (OA) Company Records, MS 508, Reel 3, v. 137, item 20, March 20, 1911, p. 20.
31. *Ibid.*, v. 144, April 3, 1912, p. 114.
32. *Toronto World*, "Robert Davies Will Filed for Probate", April 26, 1916.
33. The action was tried before Justice Lennox in the trial division of the Supreme Court of Ontario in 1917, with the plaintiff, Isabella Taylor, being represented by Wallace Nesbitt, Q.C., M.K. Cowan, Q.C. and C.C. Robinson, Q.C.; and the defendant E.R.C. Clarkson, by W.N. Tilley, Q.C. and R.H. Parmenter, all of whom were leading members of the Ontario Bar at the time.
34. "Davies Claim Void . . ." newspaper clipping, no date, no newspaper, family scrapbook.
35. At Trial, (1917), 39, *Ontario Law Reports*, 205.
36. *Ibid.*
37. His Lordship opened his remarks:

    There is no rule more relentlessly enforced than that of a trustee, purchasing the trust estate, must affirmatively establish that he fully and fairly disclosed every fact and circumstance within his knowledge which would, or might, affect the action of his trust. He must not leave the Court to speculate how much was concealed and how much was revealed. He must make it clear that he concealed nothing, and that he revealed all—he must show that he kept nothing back or the sale cannot be completed. It is immaterial whether he was a trustee only or was also interested in his own right. Here there was no attempt to sell, although a sale had been directed by the inspectors: and meantime, this inspector steps in and arranges for the conveyance to himself and thereafter acts as if it were his own property.

He concluded that: "the deed to Mr. Davies was voidable at the time he obtained it, and subject to the question of lapse of time, cannot be allowed to stand".

38. On his appeal, the defendant Davies was represented by I.F. Helmuth, K.C., and M.H. Ludwig, K.C. and Isabella Taylor by Wallace Nesbitt with Christopher Robinson. Mr. Clarkson was represented by W.N. Tilley and R.G. Parmenter. The five judges of the Appellate Court did not agree whether Davies, by reason of his duties and responsibilities as an inspector, was disabled from becoming a purchaser and they did not accept all the findings of fact made by the trial judge, but they were unanimously of the opinion that the Limitations Act applied and that action not having been brought within the period of ten years from the time of the transaction in question, it was barred by that statute.

39. At the Judicial Committee of the Privy Council in England, Isabella Taylor was represented by Sir John Simon, K.C., a leader of the English Bar and H.V. Scott, K.C., a prominent Ontario barrister, while W.N. Tilley with G. Lawrence of the English Bar appeared for Davies.

40. Lord Cave said in his reasons for judgement:

Now it is clear that the condition under which alone such a transaction can be upheld were not fulfilled. The character and prospects of the brickyard, although probably well known to the defendant, who was in possession under his agreement of tenancy, were never properly ascertained by the assignee or communicated to the creditors. It is not shown that full value was given for the property and the evidence (so far as it goes) points to the conclusion that if the property had been offered publicly a much larger price would have been obtained for it. Doubtless some of the creditors assented to the transaction but these were a small minority of the whole body, and it is doubtful whether, when they gave their assent, they did so with knowledge of the material facts. In these circumstances it appears to their Lordships that the arrangement if impeached at the time, could not have stood but must have been set aside. It is not shewn that the plaintiff only shortly before she brought her action had such knowledge of the facts as to be barred by laches or acquiescence from accepting such remedy as she may have. It follows that the true and only defence to the action is the plea of the Limitations Act.

The following may also be of interest to those concerned with the fine points of the case:

Although an action to recover trust propety still retained by a trustee is not barred under the Limitations Act either in the case of an express trustee, that is a trustee named as such in a written instrument, or in the case of a person who becomes a trustee by operation of law as in this case, their Lordships in the Privy Council decided that the expressions of "Trust Property" and "retained by the trustee" apply, not to a case where a person having taken possession of property on his own behalf is liable to be declared a trustee by the Court, but rather to a case where he originally took possession upon trust for or on behalf of others. In other words, the expressions refer to cases where a trust arose before the occurrence of the impeached transaction and not in cases where it arises only by reason of the transaction itself:

41. G. Carruthers, p. 319.
42. I. Howes, p. 24.
43. Ibid.
44. Inventory of Historical Houses, p. 28.
45. *Globe and Mail,* "Norman Davies, Bred and Raced Thoroughbreds, Won 2 Plates", December 14, 1961.
46. J.I. Rempel, *The Town of Leaside* (Toronto: East York Historical Society, 1982), p. 25.